Adrian's Fury

dpInk: DonnaInk Publications

dpInk

U.S.A.

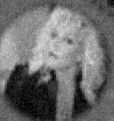

The Adrian Trilogy, Vol. II

BY LYN GIBSON

dpInk: DonnaInk Publications
www.donnaink.com

Adrian's Fury

Written By

Lyn Gibson

Copyright © 2014 by dpInk: Donnalnk Publications, L.L.C. for Lyn Gibson.
Cover art © 2014 by dpInk: Donnalnk Publications, L.L.C. created by Lyn Gibson.

Donna Ink and Company
dpInk: Donnalnk Publications, L.L.C.
The Book Nook / Donnalnk Publications (former sole proprietorship)
129 Daisy Hill Road, Carthage, NC 28327
Visit our website at www.donnaink.com

dpInk: Donnalnk Publications, L.L.C. and logo are trademarks of Donna Ink, a flagship company. The publisher is not responsible for websites (or their content) that are not owned by the publisher.

Cover Design: Ms. Lyn Gibson. Editorial Team: dpInk: Donnalnk Publications, L.L.C.: Mr. Philip Bartholomew, Mr. Quante Bryan; ZenCon an Art of Zen Consultancy, Ms. Dana Queen - Layout and Design. Final galley editorial by author.

First Paperback Edition: September 2014. First Electronic Edition: September 2014.

Library of Congress Cataloging in Publication Data

Lyn Gibson, 2014 -
Adrian's Fury / The Adrian Trilogy / by Lyn Gibson. - 1st ed.
198 p.cm.

Summary: "Christian and Adrian find themselves at the helm of a Vampire revolution as clans divide and clash. This installment of The Adrian Trilogy places readers deep within Adrian's thoughts as she evolves and strategically plots her revenge." ~ Summary by the author.

ISBN: 978-1-939425-50-8 9 (aka Print)

[1. Characters in Literature - Fiction, 2. Horror - Fiction, 3. Vampire - Fiction, 4. Fantasy Magic - Fiction, 5.Paranormal - Fiction, 6. Vampire History – Creative Nonfiction, 7. Adult Relationships - Fiction, 8. Characters - Fiction, 9. Erotica - Fiction, 10. United States - Fiction 11. Women's Literature - Fiction.]

I. Title. II. Title: Adrian's Fury, Series
PZ(1)-(4) [Fic]-dc23

2013936120

10 9 8 7 6 5 4 3 2 1

Printed in the United States of America

Table of Contents

Table of Contents i

Reviews iii

Other Titles by Lyn vii

Preface ix

Acknowledgement xi

Dedication xiii

Chapter One 1

Chapter Two 19

Chapter Three 27

Chapter Four 35

Chapter Five 43

Chapter Six 49

Chapter Seven 55

Chapter Eight 63

Chapter Nine 69

Chapter Ten 81

Chapter Eleven 89

ADRIAN'S FURY

Chapter Twelve 93

Chapter Thirteen 99

Chapter Fourteen 107

Chapter Fifteen 109

Chapter Sixteen...111

Chapter Seventeen..117

Chapter Eighteen...123

Chapter Nineteen 131

Chapter Twenty..137

Chapter Twenty-One..143

Chapter Twenty-Two 149

Chapter Twenty-Three..157

Chapter Twenty-Four...165

About the Author 173

Visit the Author..175

Mailing List and Merchandise.................................177

Reviews

TO BE HIS SOULMATE:

Mystery, romance, action...this book has it all! I loved the history intertwined in this beautiful story and the way the characters give you a little more info as the story unfolds. A must read!

~ Rachel Elp

This was a great book. I for one am not a reader. But shamelessly I have to admit this was one of the first book I have ever read that was not business or work related. I found I could not put it down. I had to make myself put it down. Great story line. This is a must read. The story line was not boring it kept you wanting to see what happened next. Loved the book and can way till the next one.

~ S. Ragan

ADRIAN'S FURY

Once I started reading this story I couldn't put it down. You are engrossed in the love story, the history, the intrigue, the excitement, and the turmoil all at the same time. Looking forward to reading the second installment!

~ Tony

This book is so beautifully written that it draws you into their time and space. I couldn't put it down. It has intrigue, passion, drama and a unique perspective on the paranormal world of the vampire in our everyday lives. It is definitely an adult's only book. I can't wait for the sequel! Don't miss out on this one!

~ T. Kenyon

Kudos for originality . . . Great storyline look forward to the next book.

~ N. Skuby

I was unable to put it down. Was very addicting. It was a new take on southern vampires. Can't wait for the next one.

~ Kim

ADRIAN'S FURY:

I must say I have never been interested in reading books regarding Vampires until now. This is the 2nd in the trilogy & I only wish the 3rd was available! Good read! Love the size of the book & the print too.

~ Rhonda Zimmerman

Had to wait for the second to come out, but I am glad I did. Great read and keeps you turning pages...then it is over. :(When is the next one coming out? Can't wait.

~ Douglas Hackworth

Awesome book!! So great, I was chomping at the bit waiting for the second book to come out. Really outstanding. Lyn Gibson is a very talented author.

~ Brittany Gibson

ADRIAN'S LEGACY:

A crazy mix of vampire lore, fantasy adventure fiction with a seductive love story and a few shades of grey!! The 1st book draws you in and then you can't put it down. The 2nd books takes off fast & furious and then you can't put it down... I haven't read the 3rd part of the trilogy yet - but I can't wait! Wasn't into Vampire stories but Lyn Gibson did an awesome job writing this series. Buy it!!!!

~ LA Reed

I have read 2 of the 3 books in this collection, must say at first it wasn't a book I would normally read. When I started reading the book I couldn't put it down. Got the second book for Christmas read it in a couple days. Have to find the time to go get the third book. Hands down one of my favorite authors. This collection is a must read.

~ Terri Liuzza

ADRIAN'S FURY

I have to say that I love any and all paranormal romances! The Adrian Trilogy did not disappoint. I am looking forward to more books by Lyn Gibson. Being able to immerse yourself in a story is what makes the story so much fun.

~ Piper

From the first book until the last page of the third book it was EXCITING & SUSPENSEFUL. Could not put down.

~ Sandra

UNBELIEVABLE!!!! The best series I have ever read! The movie is going to AWESOME!

~ John Gibson

Other Titles by Lyn

The Adrian Trilogy

✝ To Be His Soulmate

✝ Adrian's Fury

✝ Adrian's Legacy

Short and Gory

Preface

As a fanatic of Vampire legend and lore with a taste for blood and gore, *To Be His Soulmate* (Volume I) of *The Adrian Trilogy* was penned as my response to the "socialization" of the Vampire. There is little that remains valid in today's releases demonstrating the true depiction of this creatures' malevolent and vicious nature. It has all but diminished.

My quest began in 2012 with the release of, *To Be His Soulmate* — otherwise known as the first title of the *The Adrian Trilogy* series. It was intended to return the Vampire to their true state. This quest was expanded by signing with a publishing house and re-editioning, *To Be His Soulmate* (in a revised text) in 2013, which has received excellent industry reviews both nationally and internationally.

Now, is release of *Adrian's Fury, Volume II* of *The Adrian Trilogy*. True Vampire lovers from around the globe have been awaiting *Adrian's Fury*.

This, my latest title, explodes from its pages as Adrian transforms from human to immortal amidst bloody clashes between rogue clans and the Vampire Nation. Together . . . Adrian and Christian face extreme trials and tribulations. Their encounters rattle even the greatest minds of these superior beings.

"Do not fear the darkness, for you are never truly alone. Save your fear, for in it you will find strength in your greatest time of need."

Acknowledgement

First, and foremost, I am thankful for the undying patience and never ending support of my husband, John Gibson who is my biggest fan!

In addition, to all of my friends and family who have supported me during the release of *The Adrian Trilogy* including my most brutal critics and loyal fans . . . I am forever grateful!

A huge thanks to my publisher and confidant, Ms. D. L. Quesinberry, Founder and CEO of the dpInk Imprint and Donnalnk Publications, L.L.C. Thank you for believing in me and my work, and for giving me the opportunity to share it with the world!

One last note of thanks is for my best friend Jane Womack who now watches over and supports me from the great beyond. You are sorely missed Jane.

Dedication

This book is dedicated to all of the creatures of the night who have intrigued mankind since the dawn of time.

Adrian's Fury

Chapter One

Adrian strained her eyes to focus as she awoke from her extended slumber. She lay completely still, realizing there was an eerie silence within her.

One would never notice the sounds made by the mechanics of their own body until there were none. She noted no heartbeat. No sounds of a pulse rang through her ears. Weak and in pain she was none-the-less alive; at least, in some way.

Remaining motionless, Adrian listened intently to her surroundings. There was a symphony of noises vibrating throughout her. She focused on each unique sound and was able to discern immediately from what and where each sound originated. Her mind was processing information quickly, yet she was not overwhelmed. Adrian felt nothing less than odd as she became aware of new and heightened senses. These were now odd, yet comfortable. She understood this to be her new existence. Settling into this new reality, her thoughts shifted.

Adrian began to relive the last coherent moments she could recall. One by one scenes of her last mortal day flashed before her eyes. She clenched her fists tightly, shivering as she remembered laying helplessly in a pool of her own blood. There beside her lay the mangled bodies of her best friend and her pup. Their lifeless eyes stared desperately into hers as she felt her own life force slowly drain from her body. She recalled the vicious attack, which had taken place. All the bloodshed and death about her had happened so fast. She could feel Christian there with her. She still heard his cries as he pled for her to cling to the last of her life-force.

The reality that she somehow had survived began to seep into her consciousness and Adrian sensed a familiar presence in the room with her. Taking a deep breath she mustarded up the strength to roll over to see who was there. In the corner of the room sat Christian, hard at work at his desk. She lay perfectly still, curiously observing him as he worked. She saw him now as she had never seen before. She saw him both with her eyes and with a new sight, which came from deep within.

"So beautiful" she thought as she continued to study him. At once Christian sat erect in his chair sensing she had finally awoken. He sprang to his feet abruptly in hopes it was true.

"Adrian, you're awake," he whispered as if he feared had he not spoken the words they would not be true. In the blink of an eye Christian was sitting next to her. He stroked her cheek as tears of relief rolled down from his exhausted face.

"You have come back to me," he whispered as he leaned toward her while gently kissing her forehead. In a weakened motion, Adrian reached for him as he leaned into her. At a loss for words, Adrian wept for of her lost loved ones as well as for the joy of holding Christian once again in her arms.

Overwhelmed, both Christian and Adrian, lay in an embrace. Neither spoke. Neither had the necessary words to express their emotions.

Finally, Christian broke their silence, "Are you angry with me?" he whispered.

Adrian understood he referred to having turned her to Vampire to save her life. He rose to a seated position and held her hand. He awaited eagerly to hear her response.

Following Christian's face with her eyes, Adrian began to smile and looked up at him.

"No, Christian, I love you now as I loved you before," all she could manage was a whisper.

Relieved by her response, Christian felt the weight of his world lifted from his shoulders. He had great concern he had not reached Adrian in time to save her or that she would not survive turning. He also feared she would not forgive his actions on her behalf.

Christian held vigilant, remaining by her side both day and night in their darkened chamber since the attack. Having fed little, he was weakened. Adrian's response rejuvenated him.

"Are you strong enough to sit up Adrian? I can help you." Christian extended his hand and Adrian reached out to him. He lifted her to rest against their headboard in a seated position. She settled next to Christian.

"I know you will have many questions . . ." he spoke reassuringly and she nodded in return.

"Everything is the same Christian, I know this, but it is also very different. I feel a life-force moving about the house above us, for instance . . ." Adrian's voice remained a whisper.

Christian held her face, "This feeling is normal for us. It becomes second nature soon enough." His knowing glance accompanied with a still-life smile reassured her. Adrian nodded, her eyes welled with tears once more. In part, from grief; in part, from exhaustion; and in part, from realizing she was becoming overwhelmed with her internal changes.

Christian held her as she wept. "I will never leave your side. Your happiness will increase from this day forward."

Christian held her as she wept. "I will never leave your side. Your happiness will increase from this day forward."

"You should feed." Christian stood from the bed declaratively.

Numbed by his words, Adrian realized feeding had just become a necessity of an altogether different nature. She looked at Christian and for the first time in their union . . . he saw fear in her eyes. Sitting on the bed next to her once again, he sighed and collected his words.

"You are no longer mortal Adrian. This is something we all go through – you will adjust." he attempted to reassure her. "Some have more difficulty to this adjustment than others . . . I am sorry our situation has not allowed us time to prepare you for the inevitabilities of being Vampire. I promise you, we will get through this together."

Christian drew his wrist to his mouth.

Adrian closed her eyes, attempting to prepare for what she was about to do.

Christian slid her onto his lap. He placed his open wrist to her mouth. "Feed." He whispered as Adrian begrudgingly opened her mouth to receive his blood.

Adrian sucked lightly at his wrist. Soon, she came to realize as did so, she felt his blood pulse through her body. Immediately, she regained her strength and a surge of her senses exploded internally. Christian's blood sated a hunger within her she had no previous knowledge of. Her pain began to cease. She brought her hands to his, to caress Christian as she suckled. Adrian realized she was actually enjoying this feeding. After a few moments more she drew his wrist from her mouth placing a soft kiss onto his hand as she released it.

"How do you feel now?" Christian asked.

Her expression told him she was experiencing a sensation foreign to her. Adrian sat upright in their bed, "I want to stand." She made her way to the side of the bed.

Christian stood next to her. She rose to her feet and slowing steadied herself as she began to take her first steps as an immortal.

Adrian felt as though her muscles had not been used in years; however, she regained her strength at an unbelievable rate. After a few steps away from Christian she turned and walked back to him. Adrian then placed her head upon his chest.

He welcomed her with his warm embrace. "I want for you to lie back down now. You must rest." He ushered her back to their bed to rest.

As she settled, Adrian realized by ingesting Christian's blood she acquired a portion of his consciousness. His memories flashed through her mind. Eager to absorb them, she ignored the reality in doing so, she would be forced to relive the death and destruction she had last witnessed.

Christian slid into bed next to her and held her close to him, "I thought I would lose you. I feared you would be angry with me for turning you. Or worse, that you would not wake at all."

Adrian ran her hands through his tousled hair. Sighing she stated, "I would have done the same, I would have done anything I could have done to save you." Looking deeply into Christian's beautiful dark eyes, she asked . . . "How long was I asleep, what have I missed other than being in your arms?"

"You've slept for several weeks. This is longer than normal yet understandable considering what you have been through." Christian propped his head up and looked deeply at her. His statement reminded Adrian she was no longer mortal. She blurted out, "How will I ever be able to go back to work, how will I explain this to my staff?"

Christian began to chuckle at her as she had still not fully shed her mortal ways. "You have no need to work now." He grinned. "Your staff," he sighed, "have been quite difficult to handle. They have been checking up on you daily," he rubbed his brow as he finished his statement.

"Oh, I can imagine you have had your hands full with them." Adrian smiled, while asking . . . "Exactly what did you tell them?" As the question left her the smile did as well.

Christian took a deep breath; he had been anticipating this question.

Knowing there was no use in trying to hide any of the details from her, he began to relay the events he had arranged to explain her injuries as well as the death of her beloved friend Jenny. Christian rolled onto his back. He stared at the ceiling and began to explain in entirety to avoid the barrage of questioning, which he was certain would come next.

"We destroyed what remained of Daphne and her clan members and buried my men in the estate cemetery. Markus relocated Jenny's body and car to the Interstate between here and New Orleans. She was discovered the following morning by a State Trooper. I called your office the next morning and told them you had fallen and hit your head on the bar after the party. I informed them you were being kept sedated at a private facility in order for tests to be completed. Christian waited for her response.

Adrian sat quietly as she digested what she had been told. After a moment she asked, "And Oink?"

Christian rolled onto his side to face her, "I buried Oink by the cabin near the pond, I thought you would approve of the location."

Adrian nodded her head. She stared blankly and much to Christian's surprise uttered a sincere, "Thank you." She reached out to caress his handsome face. "It's going to take me a while to adjust to everything . . . be patient with me Christian." Again, she fought back the tears.

He slid in closer to her and wrapped his arms around her, "I have waited many lifetimes for you my dear. I am not going anywhere."

Christian was unaccustomed to seeing Adrian in a fragile state. She was always stubborn and independent. She now appeared frail to him, which made his love grow more deeply. He sighed as he held her close to him, happy to have her in his arms. They began to fade off into sleep together, something that they had both missed since the tragic events of that night.

Now early evening, Christian's eyes sprang open. He worried Adrian's waking may have only been a dream. He sat and looked to see Adrian rouse momentarily with his movements. Relieved, he slowly stood from their bed to contact the Vampire Council with his news. He made his way quietly to the stairwell only stopping to retrieve his cell phone from the bar on his way out.

Christian closed the passage to their suite entering the main level of the house. Eagerly he dialed Lucas . . .

"Good evening Christian" Lucas answered immediately. "Is there any change in Ms. Adrian?" he asked.

"Yes, she woke this afternoon and remembers everything. I was able to feed her briefly. Physically, she is okay but emotionally she is struggling to digest things. She is still in much pain."

Lucas sighed heavily, "I am happy to know she is doing better. As for her emotions . . . we are all here to support both of you. I will be sure to let everyone know the happy news," he added.

Christian hesitated prior to changing the subject . . . after a moment's silence he asked, "Have we heard any news on the other attacks?"

Lucas, not wanting to dampen Christian's mood answered, "Nothing good to report, Christian. We lost more men, some of those injured at the Grenoble Estate were too weak to be saved. Daphne's clan is running rampant still. With Ms. Adrian in the condition she is in presently, we are disadvantaged for tracking them, to stop them."

While nodding, Christian answered Lucas's underlying question, "It may take several days or even weeks Lucas for Adrian to recover fully. Taken into consideration of her physical and emotional traumas and experiences . . . there is nothing I can do to rush her. She has asked me to be patient with her."

"I understand Christian. We do not want you to do anything to jeopardize her. She sacrificed so much for us already; I would like to see her soon as would Ruth and Naomi. You know, they have been very worried about her. We yearn for your visit; however, it is not safe to travel at this time."

Christian hesitated, "I sense she has awakened . . . I need to go to her. We will talk again later." Ending the call abruptly, Christian rushed to their basement suite.

Adrian woke feeling stronger than she had earlier. She felt her enlightened senses grow in strength and opened her eyes to look about the room. Still overwhelmed, uncertain how to cope with this strange yet alluring sensation, she rose up to once more sit on the edge of their bed. Adrian now focused on the silence. She felt the presence of the living all around her. From the smallest of creatures beyond the walls to Christian's men vigilantly patrolling their property. Her senses became so acute she could hear the thoughts of each guard as she focused upon them. Above her, she felt Christian who was now aware she had awakened and was eager to see to her. Within moments she could see him descending the stairwell.

"Look at you!" Christian exclaimed as he saw her sitting on her own. He rushed to her and knelt at her feet. "How do you feel?" he asked as he placed his hands on her lap.

"Strange, weak, strong . . . I'm not really sure how I feel just yet. I am happy you are here to help me." Adrian replied in sheepishly declarative manner demonstrating she wasn't quite herself yet.

"How would you feel about a long hot bath?" Christian asked changing the subject to a positive note.

Adrian thought and then nodded as Christian lifted her from the bed carrying her up the stairwell to the main house. Both realized this would be Adrian's first time passing through the hallway where Jenny and Oink had been viciously murdered.

Adrian's eyes began to focus on the very spot where they had lain. She remembered the pain she felt as she looked into their lifeless eyes while her own life slipped from her. She remembered being unable to help them and unable to help herself.

Christian sensed she was becoming upset, "Everything is as it was" he whispered into her ear. She wrapped her arms tightly around his neck and thanked him for eliminating all of the evidence of what had happened. Soon after, he lay her onto her bed in her master suite while he drew her hot bath. She watched him carefully test the water for her. She thought to herself . . .

"I need to get clean clothes."

Immediately Christian blurted, "You will do no such thing, I am taking care of you!"

Realizing he heard her thoughts Adrian tested him further.

"I love you, Christian," she thought.

He stood and walked to her. He held out his hands for her to stand and pulled her close to him. "And I love you, Adrian," he said as he began to undress her.

Adrian stood weakly in front of him. Now naked, she began to wonder how badly she must look. Christian leaned to lift her, "I want to walk," she said. He hesitated, knowing to refuse her was futile and offered a compromise.

"I will help you," he said, as he offered his arm to her. She was reminded of the first date with him where she had been hesitant to take his arm and a smile crossed her face.

Slowly she walked to the bathroom and stopped to look at herself in the mirror. Surprised at what she saw, Adrian stood and stared blankly at her reflection. Her complexion was perfect, her hair long and healthy, the eyes staring back at her were weak but had a new underlying fierceness. Lastly, there was no sign of the injury she had sustained in the attack. She drew her hands to her neck in disbelief, no scar.

"Beautiful as always," Christian said as she stood gawking at herself. He turned to face her and placed a soft kiss upon her forehead then lifted her to set her into the large steaming tub. The water welcomed her and calmed her racing mind as she was submerged into it. Christian sat on the steps next to her, relishing the fact she had been returned to him.

"I am not used to you being so submissive," he smiled. "I know that you have a lot on your mind and will not pry, but please talk to me so we can get through this together," he said, as he stroked her wet shoulder with the back of his hand.

Adrian reached up and took his hand in hers, "I hurt, I am scared," she said as she turned to face him.

"I understand why you hurt, there is nothing I can do to change that, but why are you scared?" he asked as he prodded her to open herself to him.

Adrian sat for a moment and tried to sort her words. "I am something I am not used to being, I feel the abilities I had before are changing and I cannot control them. I am not used to not being in control." After a moment of deep thought she added, "I'm sure once I am back on my feet I will be able to sort through all of this and regain my normal composure. The most important thing is I have you here with me, I could have lost you too." Adrian looked into Christian's eyes, though she had been able to see his thoughts as a mortal, she could see and comprehend so much more now and it came freely to her.

Christian became a bit apprehensive as he realized even in her weakened state, he could not block her from reading his thoughts. She brought her hands to his face and drew him close to her, kissing him on his lush lips. "I look forward to spending an eternity with you," she said as she released his face to settle back down into the tub.

Christian sat smiling, but diverted his eyes from her. He hoped she had not seen any of the recent turmoil the rogue clans had initiated. In an attempt to distract her he changed the subject, "This may not be the perfect time to bring it up, but you need to feed again. The more you feed, the faster you will regain your strength."

Adrian sat quietly as she absorbed his words. Christian, taking her silence as an unspoken agreement, drew his wrist to his mouth and opened it once more for her. "Drink," he said, as he laid his arm across the tub in front of her. Adrian looked into his eyes helplessly as she knew he was right, after a moment she took his open wound into her mouth and drank from him.

She found his blood was sweet to her and realized she wanted more, but was concerned over taking too much from him and making him weak. As the realization took hold of her Christian responded, "More," he said as he coaxed her to have her fill.

Adrian continued to drink from him for a moment more and then pulled herself away. "Now you will need to feed" she said as she rinsed the blood from his closing wound. She could feel his blood rushing through her body, as if it were emitting a power surge through her as it traveled.

"You do not worry about me" Christian said, as he rolled his sleeve back down. Adrian, feeling much stronger now, stood abruptly from the tub, shocking him.

"You're feeling better now, I see," he said smiling.

She nodded as she reached for his hand to climb over the step and stand facing him. She placed her wet hand upon his chest and drew her naked body to his. Aroused and surprised by her actions, Christian stood motionless to see what her next move would be.

Adrian placed her arms around his neck and stood on tiptoe to kiss him. She gently brushed her lips against his, hesitated, and then placed a deep and passionate kiss upon his lips. He stood lost in his own passion, as they had not made love for some time. Even more aroused now, she began to place a line of kisses down his neck when suddenly she drew away from him and slapped her hand over her mouth.

She stood motionlessly holding her mouth as her eyes bulged with shock.

Christian began to chuckle at her, "Forgot about that, didn't you?" he said. "Let's see them," Christian coaxed.

Adrian turned to the mirror and slowly removed her hand to reveal her own set of protruding fangs. Slowly the shock began to leave her eyes as she realized she actually admired them.

Christian stood behind her and admired her reflection as well. "You are so beautiful," he said as he lowered his head to kiss her shoulder.

"This will prove to be a problem with wearing lipstick" Adrian smirked.

Christian's head popped up from her shoulder, surprised by her comment he began to laugh, "Ahhhhh, that's a little bit of my Adrian coming back to me" he said as he stared at her reflection affectionately.

Adrian turned to face him and raised herself onto the vanity, now seated she wrapped her legs around him and playfully drew him closer to her. Christian stroked the back of his hand down her chest following it closely with his eyes, raising his head as he reached her navel.

"Though I want nothing more than to make love to you right now, I think it best to wait until you have gained full strength and have had time to adjust to everything" he said as he looked longingly into her intense blue eyes. Adrian then pulled him even closer and placed a passionate kiss upon his lips, then laid her head on his shoulder. Christian held her tightly, stroking her hair as they stood in embrace. After a moment he backed away from her and retrieved a towel to cover her with. "Sarah!" he tolled.

In the distance Adrian heard a familiar voice.

"Yes, Mr. Christian" it rang. Soon after she could hear a heartbeat muffled by the rustling of someone entering the room. She looked up to see Sarah from the Grenoble Estate.

"Sarah, what are you doing here?" Adrian exclaimed.

"Oh, Ms. Adrian, you're awake!" Sarah gleamed. "Mr. Christian sent for me to come and take care of you. When I heard what had happened, I packed my things and came immediately, I am just so happy to see you up and about!" Sarah giggled.

Adrian looked to Christian, "You are too good to me" she said, smiling. Christian grinned broadly at her statement as he turned to Sarah.

"Help Ms. Adrian get dressed" he said as he turned to leave the room.

Adrian made her way across the room to sit on the bed. "Sarah, could you grab my pink jogging suit from the third drawer on the left, please?" she asked.

Sarah scurried across the room and gathered clothes for her, bringing an assortment of undergarments for her to select from. After laying the clothes on the bed she stood with her hands folded in front of Adrian, "Do you want for me to dress you?" she asked.

"No, that won't be necessary" she replied. Adrian realized along with hearing Sara's heart beating a strange aroma seemed to follow her. After having fed from Christian, she knew it was Sara's blood she smelled. "I assume that this is normal" she thought as she fumbled with her clothing.

"Ms. Adrian, if I may, I know there are many questions you may have now that you are a new Vampire. I have counseled many upon them having been turned. Mr. Christian thought you may find it easier to speak with me about these things than him" she said as she stared at her feet.

Adrian continued to fumble with her clothing as she began to dress. After a moment, she responded.

"I do have many questions, I just do not know how to ask them" she smiled thoughtfully. "I am thankful you came to be with us as well as volunteering to help me with this transition, I will take you up on your offer at some point" she added.

"Is there anything I may get for you?" Sarah asked. Adrian thought for a moment, realizing other than feeding on Christian she had not eaten, but was not hungry and could not think of any one thing she had any desire for. Adrian, in order to have a moment of privacy, decided to ask Sarah for a glass of wine. Sarah bowed her head slightly and eagerly scurried from the room to fill her request.

She, now dressed, walked to her patio doors to view her grounds. Adrian noted the guards she had sensed earlier as they patrolled around her home. She also noticed they were all dressed in military attire and were heavily armed. She had remembered Christian's previous security force dressed in suits, and at that moment she realized the threat had not fully passed. Adrian began to stare into the dark tree line at the back of the property, straining to recall the scene outside of the house on the night of the attack.

Slowly she began to see the events as they had occurred; though dim and fuzzy, Adrian was able to determine how the assassins had originated their attack. One by one, she watched as Christian's security team was ripped apart. She tried to block the sound of their desperate wailing in order to concentrate on the faces of the evil intruders that busied themselves by scattering the remains of their prey about the grounds. Daphne stood dominantly on the back lawn as she ordered teams of assassins to left and right of the property, taking the remainder of them with her through the very door that Adrian was looking out of.

Daphne's face was riddled with venom as she approached the door. With a flick of the wrist the patio doors flung open and Daphne was inside of her home. She began to grow angry as she saw Daphne walk through the door and into the hall. Though she still stood staring into the tree line, Adrian saw the attack as if she were standing behind Daphne. Suddenly she saw Daphne's head swing to the left. Adrian realized that was the moment that her pup had tried to attack.

Adrian clenched her eyes closed as she knew the outcome of the event, but still the scene continued to play on. Her eyes filled with tears as she watched her pet slam into the wall and slide to the floor in a mangled and bloody heap. Then Daphne had turned her sights on Jenny. Adrian's body shuddered as she relived the sight of her friend's brutal death. She watched on as Daphne fed on Jenny then ripped her throat from her body. As Jenny's body slumped to the floor, Adrian could see herself in Daphne's path and began to prepare, as she knew what was to come. The vision was so vivid that she could smell the powder from the gun blast. As smoke billowed into the air, she could see the pellets scatter as they grazed Daphne's head. Adrian was paralyzed by the vision. She clinched her fists and watched the blood splatter from her own throat as Daphne ripped her open in rebuttal. Her body fell to the floor and now she could see Christian charging towards Daphne. With fangs bared, he began to rip Daphne open, slicing her wider with every blow. Adrian studied Christian in his wild state, as she focused on the fury in his eyes, her concentration was broken by the sound of Sarah entering the room.

Sarah stood gawking as she gripped the glass of wine she'd requested. Adrian realized her feet were not touching the floor; startled, she suddenly dropped back to the floor, steadying herself as she landed.

"Deep in thought you were, I see," Sarah said as she walked to Adrian to hand her the glass of wine. Adrian accepted the glass and sat it onto the nightstand next to her. "Thank you, Sarah" she said, as she attempted a polite smile.

"These things happen, Ms. Adrian, though not usually this quickly. No worries, you will learn to control them in time." Sarah smiled warmly. "Tell me, what were you thinking just now?" Sarah coaxed.

Adrian retrieved the glass of wine and walked to the bed to sit across from Sarah. As she settled, she took a deep breath and began to explain the vision she had experienced. Sarah nodded in understanding and walked to Adrian.

"May I?" she said as she motioned to the spot next to her on the bed.

Adrian nodded as she sipped at her wine.

"Because of the abilities you had in your mortal life and because of the stature of your maker, you will become quite strong." Sarah began. "You will learn to master these skills, as they are not completely new to you, only stronger than what you knew before. Having known you before the transition, I have all confidence in you adapting well," she finished. Sarah stood and smiled down at Adrian, "If there is nothing else you need from me for the evening, I will retire in order to give you and Mr. Christian your privacy."

Adrian nodded in response, "Thank you, Sarah, for everything, have a good evening."

Sarah smiled reassuringly and turned to leave the room.

Adrian continued to sit on the bed while she absorbed Sarah's advice. She took another sip of her wine and noted the flavor was different now that her senses were enhanced. She could taste not only the fruit but the earth it had been grown in as well. She stood from the bed and made her way into the living room to find Christian sitting at the bar enveloped in an in-depth conversation. He raised his head and smiled broadly at her as she sat down across from him.

"Adrian is here with me now, we will discuss this further later" he said as he ended his call.

"How are you?" he said as he reached across the bar for her hand.

"I'm feeling stronger" she responded. Adrian took a deep breath to continue, hesitated, and then decided to tell him of what she had seen.

"After I was dressed, I walked to the patio doors to look around outside. I felt drawn to look to the tree line at the back of the property. The sight seemed to trigger something within me; I was able to see the entire attack as it was happening."

She hung her head and fought to compose herself. "I saw everything all over again."

Christian stood, walked over to her and held her as she continued to describe the events as she had witnessed them. When she finished, she turned to face him and said, "I know that the threat has not passed - what exactly is going on right now?"

Christian was unable to look away from her, he was completely entranced by her eyes; he grew concerned she, as a new vampire, was advancing too quickly. He also knew he would have to completely brief her on the ongoing situation. Christian sighed as he sat next to her and began, "The attack that occurred here was one of four executed simultaneously: The Grenoble estate, the Seattle estate, the Berlin estate, and here" he sighed.

"Daphne's clan knows we were involved in destroying her plot and have continued their plot to overthrow the Parliament, as well as any clan that does not support them. We have had great difficulty in trying to track them, as they had been preparing for this for some time. We knew nothing about it until you were involved." Christian stood and began to pace the room.

Adrian listened attentively to the details that Christian was now laying in front of her. After a moment, she thoughtfully tilted her head and said, "I have got to get my strength back so I can help end this."

Christian hung his head because he knew she was right; he knew they would have to rush her recovery.

Adrian began to ponder the concept of feeding, as she knew that this would be a big part of her recovery. She knew she could not continue to feed from Christian, as it would weaken him, something that would not be wise in these perilous times. She watched as Christian paced the floor, knowing he was concerned about rushing her.

She walked to him and wrapped her arms around him. "I will adjust quickly, I will be just fine." Adrian thought while embracing him.

Christian responded with a sigh. He held her close to him. She could sense he was apprehensive about something.

"What is it you do not want to tell me?" she asked, as she stood back to look into his eyes.

Christian returned her gaze and answered, "I will need to travel soon. I have been struggling with what would be safest, to take you with me or not."

Adrian knew because of his position it was necessary for him to go and meet with the clans in person. She now began to pace, deep in thought. She knew Christian was needed elsewhere, and in his absence she knew she could push herself harder to recover. She abruptly turned to him and said, "I know you don't want to leave me, but it is important you go to the other clans. I will stay here." She ended her response as abruptly as she began.

Christian seemed surprised by her answer, "Are you sure?"

Adrian walked towards him to face him, "I do not want to be separated from you, but if we cannot get the other clans organized soon, these attacks will continue and worsen. It would be selfish of me to keep you here with me when lives could be saved" she ended.

Christian smiled. Her position on the matter made him proud. "I will leave tomorrow, and try to come back to you within a couple of days" he said begrudgingly.

Adrian nodded, "You should call Lucas and tell him so the Parliament can begin to make arrangements for you to meet with all of the leaders."

Christian walked back to the bar, picked up his phone and began to dial.

Adrian made her way to the living room and out of habit turned on the television immediately. She stared blankly at the local news anchor as she rambled on. She pondered how she would be able to live with herself feeding on other humans. The realization struck again, she was not human, she was now something far more, and would have to adjust her thinking process. She ran her hand across her brow, her thoughts interrupted by the news anchor's excited voice.

"We have just been informed the bodies of the two missing children have been found. The police have positively identified their remains and are searching for this man as a suspect in their disappearance." As the anchor continued to speak a picture of the man was displayed.

Adrian looked into the man's eyes and began to see the pain and suffering he had inflicted on the two children as well as several others. She shook off the visions as the camera shot returned to the excited anchor, "Anyone with any information on the whereabouts of this man, please call Crimestoppers" and then the anchor babbled on.

Adrian knew how she would select those she fed on; a smile crossed her face as she recalled a conversation she had had with Christian on the topic when she was human. Pleased with her decision, she stood from the couch and began to look for her laptop so she could do more research on the wanted man. "This bastard deserves to die" she thought.

Christian was still heavily involved in his conversation with Lucas and did not notice her moving about the room. She found her laptop in her office where she had left it and carried it back into the living room to begin her research. Finding a photograph of the suspect, she began to stare into his eyes and focus, straining to see if she could make out any of his surroundings. Lulling herself into a deep trancelike state, she found herself standing behind the man in a small, dimly-lit hotel room. She scanned around the room for any signs of the actual location. She shadowed behind the man as he made his way to the bed, there on the nightstand she saw a comment card.

The Camellias along with a local address was inscribed across the top of the card. Adrian smiled to herself and turned to see what the man was doing. As she did, he stood and walked away from the bed; aimed directly in her path, the man seemed to walk through her. She could see the horrible things he had done. She counted his victims' faces as they flashed before her 7, 8, 9 she counted. Momentarily distracted by the hopeless wails of each child, Adrian's heart sank and she became furious.

"Enjoy your last night on earth, you piece of shit" she thought to herself. The man returned to the bed and settled in as he stared at the ceiling. Adrian's blood boiled and she became eager to meet the man face-to-face. Concerned Christian would sense her anger, he began to calm herself to search for more information.

She began to walk towards his door and then through it. She turned to face the door and saw the number 17. Now confident on his whereabouts, she shook herself back from the trance she had submerged herself in. Normally she would have been drained from doing this in the past, but now she felt empowered and was shocked at the amount of information she had been able to gain. She closed her laptop and stood to be near Christian, who was wrapping up his droning conversation with Lucas.

Christian could sense a change in her demeanor immediately. "What have you been doing over there?" he asked.

Adrian smiled and answered, "Adjusting to becoming Vampire." She could feel him trying to pry his way into her thoughts. She imagined a set of steel doors within her mind then slammed them closed.

Christian jumped suddenly. "You are learning quickly" he said smiling.

Adrian returned his smile and reached for him, "So you are leaving tomorrow for sure?" she asked in an attempt to avoid more questioning.

"Yes" he answered, as he turned on the stool to face her.

She pried his knees open and moved closer to him. "I do not anticipate being gone for more than two days, three at the most." In the meanwhile, I have called for the security staff at my estate to be relocated here to watch over you" he ended.

Adrian nodded "Thank you" she said as she placed her hands on either side of his face.

"You are feeling stronger" Christian replied.

"I am" she answered as she drew his beautiful face to hers to place a kiss on his lips.

He responded affectionately as he lifted his hands to run his fingers through her lush blonde hair.

Adrian could feel he was becoming aroused and lifted his head so she may kiss his neck. Now aroused herself, Christian slowly drew himself back from her,

"Don't start anything that you can't finish" he said as he looked longingly into her eyes.

Adrian leered back at him, and climbed onto his lap, gently pulling his head back by his hair for her to kiss him more passionately. She could feel his manhood beginning to pulse beneath her and longed to make love to him.

Christian was nearly breathless at this point. He stood holding her up as she wrapped her legs around his waist.

"Take me to bed" she whispered in his ear, as he aggressively kissed her neck.

Christian began to make his way to the opening of their downstairs suite. As he began his descent, she began to remove her shirt and placed her bare chest on to his. He shuddered as he stroked her naked back with his hands.

Christian sat on the edge of the bed with Adrian still perched in his lap. Gently he moved his hands to her breasts, softly caressing them before placing one of them in his mouth. He sucked gently at her as she stroked his hair. Christian's breathing became labored. She stood from him and removed the remainder of her clothing. He pulled her back to him and placed his face to her stomach.

"I was terrified I had lost you" he said as he gingerly placed a kiss near her navel.

Adrian smiled, "My Christian, I will never leave you" she whispered. "Even as my mortal life fought to remain with me, I wanted nothing more than to reach out and hold you" she whispered as she held him to her.

Christian raised his head and looked into her eyes as he stood; he knew that there was an eternal truth to her vow.

Adrian began to undress him before he stood completely erect, kissing his chest as she exposed his skin. She unbuckled his belt and removed his slacks slowly as she admired his beautiful body. Christian stood submissively while she placed a line of kisses from his chest and down his stomach as she knelt before him. She eagerly took his manhood into her mouth and began to suck gently at him.

Christian placed his hands on his head and moaned in ecstasy while she stroked her mouth over him. After a moment, he drew his hands down to her and lifted her face to him, his fangs protruding as he panted. Adrian brushed her bare breasts against him as she stood. Christian's hands lovingly roamed about her body as he lifted her and placed her gently into their bed.

She caressed his broad shoulders as his head descended her body leaving a trail of passionate kisses in its wake. She trembled as his warm tongue caressed her clitoris, rousing her own fangs to emerge in passion. She ran her tongue across them as she opened her legs wide for him. Christian continued to suck at her until she was stricken with a climax more intense than she had ever known. She clutched at the linens beneath her, shredding them with her fingernails. She screamed out as her body was wracked with ecstasy. As her orgasm withered, they plunged back down onto the bed.

She and Christian exploded in laughter. "I'm surprised that security isn't beating on the door after that" Adrian giggled.

Christian laughed in response as he flipped them both over, leaving her straddling him.

She looked into his deep, dark eyes and caressed his face as she mounted herself onto him. Gently she began to raise and lower herself onto his throbbing cock. Christian pulled at his hair as he closed his eyes. She was entranced by his beautiful face; she labored lovingly as she lavished in his pleasure. His only option in avoiding climax was to quickly roll them over, he now on top of her. He looked down into her face and raised his hand to run his fingertips down her protruding fangs. Adrian, her eyes locked into his, smiled as she drew her legs up and wrapped them tightly around him. He sighed as she drew him more deeply into her, rocking his hips with hers. She spread her legs widely to welcome him as he thrust himself into her. She found herself nearing climax once more as he slowly and deeply slid in and out of her. She watched as he bit his lip and began to climax with her. Their bodies rose from the bed as they were both overcome by the ecstasy they shared.

Adrian fought the urge to bite Christian's neck as her body pulsed with his.

He seemed to have read her thoughts; "Bite me" he grunted.

Adrian complied immediately as she sank her fangs into his shoulder, seeming to enhance his orgasm. Christian screamed as he clawed at her back, in turn enhancing her climax. Moments later they were flung back into the bed a second time.

Now exhausted, he lay atop her, twisting his fingers through her hair as he attempted to catch his breath. Her chest heaved beneath his head as she gently wrapped her legs around him.

He began to lift his head from her, but she quickly wrapped her arms around his neck and drew him back to her. "I don't want for you to move" she said, still breathless. "I want to hold you while you are still inside of me" she finished.

Christian laid his head back down and began to caress her breast.

She placed her hand on top of his. "I love making love to you" she said, as she realized she was becoming aroused by the touch of his hands. She began to lightly trace his back with her fingertips. He groaned at her touch, she could feel his manhood begin to stir once more. She in turn began to throb excitedly around him in anticipation of a second round.

Christian began to rock his hips slowly as she followed his lead. He moaned with each stroke wrapping his arms tightly around her as it became obvious that he would explode shortly.

She spread her legs and placed her hands on his ass to slow his pace. She thrust slowly and deeply beneath him. Once more they met each other in a second orgasm.

"Christian!" she howled, as she threw her head back gasping. Both of them began to moan with each slow and steady stroke, "Feed . . . from . . . me," Christian managed to grunt out. Once more Adrian sank her fangs into his shoulder and sucked gently as his blood flowed into her mouth. Christian wailed as he exploded with her. His body trembled as he lay on top of her; he now completely spent.

She held his head to her chest as she massaged his temples, and soon after, both of them were sound asleep in one another's arms.

Christian awoke still in her arms. Slowly, he began to raise himself so as not to disturb her. Quietly, he stood from the bed and made his way to the shower, having just enough time to clean up and make way to his estate in New Orleans to prepare for his flight out. Now dressed, he sat by her side and gently stroked her cheek. She stirred at his touch.

"Christian" she sighed as she opened her eyes to see him. Realizing he had showered and dressed, she knew that he was now ready to leave. She sat up in the bed and leaned to kiss him brushing her lips softly against his.

"I have little time to make it to the jet. The sooner I leave, the sooner I can return to you" he sighed.

She knew he dreaded leaving her and was concerned for her safety, "I will miss you so much" she said as she draped her arms around his shoulders and pulled him to her. "Call me often" she said as she released him. Having been more concerned for him being exposed to the coming sunrise, she chose to help him keep his goodbye a brief one. Her heart sank as he stood from the bed and made his way to the door, he leaned to pick up his briefcase as he turned to look at her pretty face once more before ascending the stairwell. She listened as the opening slid shut on its tracks and the sounds of his footsteps faded away.

Adrian fell back into the bed as worry filled her mind; she was not worried for her own safety, but for his. Her mind, busy with thoughts of Christian and the plans she had for the approaching evening, prevented her from finding sleep again.

Now surely daybreak had come. She rose from the bed and made her way to the shower. The warm water trickled over her body, in turn washing her thoughts away, but only briefly.

Now showered and dressed, she made her way to Christian's desk and began to research her target further. She grew angry as she stared into the face of the vicious murderer, fueling her to see her way to draining him dry and snapping his neck. Adrian stood and walked away from the monitor just as the phone rang. She grabbed the phone to see Christian's number flash across the display.

"Missing you terribly" she answered.

Christian's warm voice melted her as he chuckled, "How are you?"

"I'm fine" she sighed into the phone. "Are you in flight yet?" she asked.

"Yes, we lifted off about 20 minutes ago, I wanted to tell you that the additional security staff should be arriving within the hour."

"Where will you be staying?" she asked as she picked up a cigarette and examined it closely.

"I will be with the Parliament, they were able to arrange several meetings while I'm there."

"Is Markus with you?" she asked.

"Yes, he is" I have left William in charge of you and the security staff; he is already there" Christian added.

"Tell Markus I said "Hello," she responded.

"Indeed I will, there are a great many details to get in order before we land, I just needed to hear your voice before we started" he whispered.

"I love you, Christian, please don't take any unnecessary risks while you are away" she said as she felt that the call was drawing to an end.

"The same goes for you; I love you Adrian" he said as he ended the call.

She sighed as she laid the phone back onto the table next to the bed. Now all there was for her to do was wait for nightfall. Adrian sank into the couch and turned the television set on to lose herself in a movie while she waited. After a while, the sound of the entrance sliding back from its tracks startled her. Adrian stood and prepared to defend herself. Suddenly a knock came to the door.

"Ms. Adrian?" Sarah's voice rang out, "May I come in?" she asked.

"Yes, Sarah" she answered. She could hear the sound of the entrance closing as Sarah opened the door.

"I wanted to come and check in on you, so sad Mr. Christian had to leave you so soon after your' awakening" Sarah said in a concerned tone.

Adrian looked to Sarah, "Thank you so much for taking care of me Sarah" Adrian said as she smiled warmly.

"There is something I want you to do Sarah. Can you call and order the same shutters for my windows as those that were on the ones at the Grenoble estate? I cannot bear to be confined in this small space" she added.

Sarah nodded in confirmation. "I will call someone first thing in the morning, in the meanwhile is there anything I can get for you Ms. Adrian?" She stood patiently with her hands folded before her as she waited for a response.

Adrian thought for a moment and responded, "Upstairs in my closet you will find several cocktail dresses. Select several with matching shoes, pack up my vanity and bring those things to me along with a bottle of wine."

Sarah looked at Adrian questioningly, but nodded her head and retreated to the stairwell without asking for more information. A short while later Sarah returned with the requested items and entered the suite. As she laid the wardrobe onto the bed, she turned to Adrian and asked, "Will you be going out this evening?"

Adrian took a deep breath and chose her words carefully as she responded to the question, "I need to heal quickly, I am needed to help end this vicious war. I have found a way to feed I feel I can live with, but if you don't mind, I do not want to comment any further on the details" she finished.

Sarah nodded and smiled weakly, "Will there be anything else?" she asked.

"No, thank you, Sarah" she answered as she watched Sarah make her way back to the stairwell and disappear into the darkness.

Chapter Two

Adrian stared into the mirror as she applied her makeup and curled her hair. It was nearly sundown. She was eerily quiet as she planned her feeding strategy for the evening.

Pleased with the outcome, she stood from the vanity and chose a revealing cocktail dress from the selection Sarah had fetched for her earlier that day. She stealthily slid into the low cut silk dress and chose a pair of stiletto heels to finish out her wardrobe then checked the time once more before accessing the stairwell.

As she entered the main floor, she saw Sarah sitting on the couch folding laundry. "Good evening Sarah" she pronounced as she walked towards the den.

Sarah stood abruptly, "Good evening, Ms. Adrian, you look stunning! But are you sure that you are well enough to leave the house?" she asked with a concerned tone.

Adrian smiled as she looked around, "I feel fine Sarah. The house looks wonderful, thank you for your hard work" she said as she reached for her keys and her purse. "Don't wait up" she added as she opened the door to leave. Sarah, still surrounded by laundry, was now deeply concerned over Adrian's safety.

As she opened her car door, she noticed that all of the security team had stopped in their tracks and were staring blankly at her. She smiled as she knew they were admiring her appearance, "I'll be back shortly" she announced as she sat behind the steering wheel and started the car.

William ran to the car before she could put it in gear. "Ms. Adrian, you are not supposed to leave the grounds" he said as he tapped on the window.

Adrian rolled her eyes and lowered the window. "William, I am going to feed, I hardly think you would want to accompany me." Feeling she may have responded a bit brashly, she added, "I have your number if I were to need you, I will return shortly" she said as she began to raise the window. William stood with his mouth agape not knowing how to reply. He stepped back from the car as Adrian proceeded to drive to the gate.

It felt like ages since she had left her home. The freedom of the rural highway beckoned to her, and she opened her sunroof to enjoy the cool night air as she drove towards town. She began to focus on her target to determine if he was still where she had last seen him. After a moment, she found herself standing in the same hotel room, watching him sleep. She grinned sneeringly as she anticipated seeing the horror in his eyes while she fed on him.

Soon she found herself pulling into the parking lot of the hotel. She drove around the building until she found the door with "17" posted on it. She sat and stared at the door for a moment and then backed into a nearby parking space, peering into the rear-view mirror to check her makeup before leaving the car. She focused on the faces of the target's helpless victims as they screamed in horror, priming herself for what she was about to do. She watched as he raped them and then cut their tiny bodies into pieces while they were still alive. She knew that replaying the scenes in her mind would make her furious and help her to complete her task.

Adrian stood from the car and made her way to the door. She took a deep breath and knocked. After a moment, she could hear movement in the room. The curtain beside the door moved as she could feel him looking at her. The door began to open, and she saw him standing behind it, scanning the parking lot before opening it fully.

"I am so sorry to bother you, but I can't get my car to crank and I'm late for a party, would it be too much to ask you to take a look at it?" Adrian poured on the Southern charm as the man stood leering at her.

"Sure," he said smiling, "Come inside while I put my shoes on and we'll see what we can do to get you on your way" he said as a filthy grin emerged upon his face.

Adrian smiled broadly, "Thank you so much! You are so kind to help me. I hate traveling alone> It seems something like this always happens to me when I am alone."

The man's smile grew into an evil grimace as he closed the door behind her and locked it. Adrian looked at him as the bolt slid shut, "Why are you locking the door?" she asked as she toyed with him.

"Oh, it's a safety precaution for me" he answered.

"For you?" she asked with a nervous tone in her voice.

"Yes, I wouldn't want for anyone to see what is about to happen to you" he said as he sprang towards her.

Adrian, still toying with him, gasped and threw her purse to the floor, "Here's my purse, you can have everything in it, just please don't hurt me!" she begged.

"I love it when they beg me" he said as he pulled a knife from his beltline. He sprang forward and grabbed her by the throat. As his hand touched her skin, she could once again see the faces of his victims, crying out for justice. Adrian became enraged.

"Does it make your dick hard when they beg you for their life or is it you need to fuck a helpless child in order to get your rocks off? You filthy motherfucker!" Adrian growled. She could feel his pulse accelerating, her fangs protruded as she could smell the fear laced adrenaline emitting from her prey. The man, dumb-founded by her comments, took a step back from her to regain his composure, as he clumsily held the knife still at her throat.

"Shut up whore" he screamed.

Adrian grabbed the wrist of his hand that held the knife. She squeezed and twisted until she heard it snap. He fell to his knees in shock and in pain as she stood over him, laughing.

"This is how it feels to strike horror into the soul of those you are about to murder" she said as she reached for his neck. "You will now know the terror you have inflicted upon your' victims as now you are my victim" she growled as she lifted him above her with one hand. Adrian was surprised by her new strength but remained focused.

The man was paralyzed with fear; his eyes bulged from his head as beads of sweat ran down his face.

Adrian bared her fangs at him as she ripped his shirt from his body. "Do you enjoy feeling helpless?" Do you enjoy knowing that you are about to experience a merciless death?" she sneered. Before he could beg for his life, she jerked him towards her and sank her fangs into his neck. She drank from him until his body fell limp.

"I will show you more mercy than you showed your prey" she whispered into his ear. She lowered him to the floor until his knees were beneath him, placed her hands on his face and stared deeply into his eyes, "Off to Hell with you!" she snarled as she twisted his neck. Adrian watched as his body slumped to the floor.

She stood staring blankly at him, surprised she had no remorse for having taken a human life. His filthy blood now pulsed throughout her body, she closed her eyes as a powerful new sensation momentarily overwhelmed her. Something similar to a rush of adrenalin shot through her body, strengthening her both mentally and physically. Adrian lavished in the sensation even as the horrific scenes of the man's memories flashed before her.

After having acclimated to the after effects of her feeding, Adrian walked into the bathroom to clean the blood from her face, careful to leave no trace of her ever having been there. She stopped at the door to examine her prey once more, then turned to make her way back to her car.

Adrian felt a new sense of pride after having fed on her own for the first time. She was exhilarated, feeling even stronger, her senses even more acute. "If I can do this for the next two nights while Christian is gone, I will be at full strength upon his return" she thought.

She now had a deeper understanding of the strength and knowledge Christian possessed. She wondered how many centuries it had taken for him to bridle his power. Her thoughts drifted to him; would he be proud of her actions of would he be angered she had disregarded his wishes and left the estate without him there to watch over her? It had been a few hours since she had heard from him. She was missing him but did not try to focus on him as he would not need the distraction while meeting with the clan leaders in these perilous times. "I will call him when I am home" she thought aloud.

Soon after she was pulling back into the gate, she parked her car and walked in to find Sarah asleep on the couch. "Sarah" she said as she patted her on the hand, "Sarah, what are you doing asleep on the couch?" Adrian laughed.

Sarah stood groggily and smiled, "I know you said not to wait up, but I had to know that you made it home alright."

"Thank you Sarah, now go get in bed and get your rest" Adrian chuckled.

Sarah nodded and walked towards the hallway. She turned before going into her room. "Ms. Adrian, I called tonight, the people will be here tomorrow to measure for the shutters, and they say they can complete the job by the week's end"

"That's good news" Adrian said as she slid the stiletto heels from her feet before walking over to sit on the couch. She sat quietly for a moment in order to compose herself before dialing Christian's number. She hoped that he would not sense what she had done; there were far more important matters in need of his attention right now.

"Hello my love" he answered.

Adrian smiled as the sound of his voice seemed to pulse through her body. "I was worried about you, I haven't heard from you since early this morning" she sighed.

"I'm sorry, time got away from me but we have made a lot of progress since I arrived" he explained. "How are you feeling?"

"I'm fine, just missing you" she answered.

There was a moment of silence before he spoke again, "I sense you are stronger; that means that you have fed, is this true?"

Adrian drew a deep breath, now knowing she could not hide the fact from him she answered, "I did; I found a way I can deal with it. I know I have to recover quickly, so I figured out what to do."

"You left the house?" he asked testily.

"Yes" she answered sheepishly as she sensed his frustration.

Christian sighed heavily, "I told William not..."

She cut him off before he could finish. "William could not have stopped me when I was mortal, he certainly could not have stopped me tonight" she teased. "He is not happy about my leaving either. Please do not be angry with him, or me" she added.

After a moment of silence, Christian spoke again. "I can hardly be mad at you; in fact, on second thought, I am quite proud of you."

She was both shocked and relieved to have heard him say this. "Thank you, that means a lot to me."

"So tell me, what it is you have found to help you deal with feeding?"

Adrian smiled, "Something I saw on the news last night made me remember what you said when I asked you about feeding on humans. Do you remember what you told me?" she asked.

"Yes, I told you that some humans don't deserve to live."

"That's right, I removed an evil man from the world tonight" she boasted. "I fed on him until he was nearly drained and then I snapped his neck" she said, matter-of-factly.

After another moment of silence Christian laughed loudly, "I knew you would adapt quickly, but not this quickly! You never fail to amaze me, Adrian."

She could sense that he was proud of her accomplishment. Now relieving her concerns of having been a distraction to him, she decided to speak more frankly. "I know how important it is I regain my strength and master my new abilities. I know that I am needed and I am striving to get to that point for all of us."

Adrian could hear other voices coming near to Christian, "I have to go now; we will talk about this later" he said hurriedly as the line went dead.

"Phone skills!" Adrian laughed as she flung her phone back onto the table.

She smiled to herself as she imagined Christian relaying their conversation to Lucas and the rest of the Parliament. Just after midnight, Adrian decided to make the most of the remainder of the night. She walked into her bedroom and changed out of her silk dress. The full moon beyond the French-doors seemed to call to her.

Adrian walked out onto the patio, her eyes raised up to the clear night sky. She filled her lungs with the cool night air as she focused her new sight into the heavens; seeing in a way that no mortal could comprehend.

She became consumed for a moment, as she continued to stare toward the moon she began to focus on the sounds of the night creatures that surrounded her; creatures that had been there all along but seldom experienced by humans.

Adrian closed her eyes as she focused on the movement around her and suddenly sensed something large moving beyond the tree line several yards away from her. She soon realized it was a young fawn.

Adrian slowly opened her eyes and peered into the direction of the deer. She was now eager to test her new abilities. She closed her eyes and set out into a full sprint as she imagined herself at her destination; within a breath she found she was standing there.

Shocked, she turned and looked back toward the house, she closed her eyes and imagined standing at the patio door. When she opened her eyes, she found that she was there. "Oh, I see" Adrian said grinning.

She decided to try for the cabin, closed her eyes for a moment and focused on the front porch before she set off again. Within only a matter of seconds she stood in front of the cabin.

Now from the cabin to the front gate, again she closed her eyes and focused. Suddenly, she stood face to face with a guard. He jumped back and fumbled for his weapon.

"You must always be on guard!" Adrian said as she turned to walk away, laughing under her breath. Deciding to test how far away she could transport herself, she walked to the front door and retrieved her phone, just for good measure.

She closed her eyes and focused on her office in town. Shortly after, she found herself standing in front of her desk.

Adrian's experiments had now nearly drained her, however, there was no better way to know the limits of her abilities than to push herself.

She slunk down into her old leather chair behind the desk and began glancing at old Post-It notes and business cards. She realized this would no longer be a part of her life. Saddened by abandoning fond memories of her staff, she closed her eyes and focused on home.

Moments later, she found herself walking on the rural highway just outside of town, breathless and nearly depleted. She walked for a little way, and then decided to call William. She continued to walk in order meet up with him more quickly.

Being completely familiar with this stretch of highway, Adrian closed her eyes and focused on a road sign that she knew to be a couple of miles ahead. She transported herself in short spurts until she saw William driving towards her.

William pulled the car up beside her. Adrian hurriedly opened the back door and climbed in before William could exit the car to do so. She slid into the back seat and sat silently, pondering the limits of her abilities.

Her deep thoughts were soon disrupted; she sensed William was irritated with her for having left the grounds a second time. Adrian attempted to avoid making eye contact with him as he pulled the car to the shoulder of the road then turned around and headed back home. He glanced over his shoulder towards her several times. She knew that they would not make it back home without having to address the situation. He chose to remain silent, much to her relief until just before pulling up to the gate.

"Ms. Adrian" he began cautiously. "I fear Lord Christian will be angry with me for failing to watch over you. I realize you do not answer to me, but I answer to Lord Christian" he continued. "I have never once let him down in all of my years of service; May I ask a favor of you?"

Adrian smiled slightly as she looked up into the mirror and into William's eyes, "Of course William" she responded.

"I understand you will not always want for me to be with you, but will you at least tell me when you leave the grounds?" he asked sheepishly.

Adrian nodded at his request, "Of course William, I apologize for putting you in this position. Lord Christian has the utmost confidence in you, as do I, this will not happen again" she finished.

"Thank you Ms. Adrian" he bowed as he pulled the car through the gate.

Once home, Adrian retreated to her suite, showered and lay in bed to rest as soon the morning sun would light the sky.

Chapter Three

Adrian slept soundly, with no regrets of the events from the previous evening. She woke feeling recharged, though she had weakened herself the night before. She rolled over and retrieved her phone from the nightstand to see if she had missed any calls from Christian. "Nothing," she sighed.

Beginning to worry about his safety, she fought the urge to call him, as it was not yet mid-day and he was likely resting. After a moment, she returned the phone to the nightstand and decided to light a cigarette.

Adrian stood and stretched then began to pace the suite. She made her way to the couch and turned on the TV in hopes of finding local news in search of another opportunity like the one she encountered the day before. With no luck, she decided to take another approach and study the local newspaper online for the past seven days. On the third day back she saw a headline, "Man sought for questioning in murder of wife and two children."

"There's my bitch!" she exclaimed.

Adrian began to research the wanted man's name, "Joshua Weston" she whispered as she typed it into the search bar. There were results immediately.

Weston appeared to have a long criminal history but had never been convicted; assault, DUI's, suspect in the disappearance of two young women, and the list went on. Finally, she was able to turn up a recent photo, just what she needed to help her locate him.

Adrian peered into his eyes, and began to see the atrocities he had committed. Weston had led a life of violence; he was guilty of far more horrific acts than what he had been suspected of. She immediately saw the faces of several young girls, which she now knew to be buried in a field just a few miles north of her.

It seemed Weston, who was aroused by torturing his victims for extended periods of time, would bring his prey within moments of death before raping them. He found great pleasure in climaxing as his victim took their last and dying breath.

"Sick Bastard," Adrian mumbled as she strained to focus on him. Moments later a vision of his surroundings began to materialize before her. She was able to make out an old green Buick parked in a wooded area. He was asleep in the back seat. She scanned the car to see if there was any clue of where he was, but there was nothing yet somehow she sensed he was not far away.

She decided to try something different. She envisioned herself placing her hand on his head and trying to read his thoughts. Much to her surprise, snapshots of where he had been the previous night flashed before her eyes. "Where are you going tonight?" she asked with her hand still on his forehead.

She began to see a man behind a bar, above his head hung a sign that said "Shorty's." There was sports memorabilia from a local college and several D.O.T. workers with Parish emblems on their sleeves. Adrian smiled. "Gotcha!" she growled under her breath.

After a little more research she was able to locate the bar, within an hour's drive of her home. Adrian began to plot his demise. She would go there and wait for his green Buick make its appearance. With all of the evening's details planned out, now she would try to contact Christian.

Christian's phone rang until his voice mail picked up. This was the first time she had ever called him and he did not answer. "Missing you and now worried; please call me when you can" she said. Adrian stared blankly at the phone; surely it would ring at any second, she thought. A few minutes later, she decided to text him. "Please call me" her message read. Several minutes passed with no response.

Adrian started pacing the length of the suite, an overwhelming sense of dread began to well up inside of her. "Markus" she said aloud, as she scrolled through her contacts to find his number. Moments later, she was eagerly awaiting Markus to answer.

"Hello?" his droning voice tolled.

"Markus, its Adrian, where is Christian?" she asked. There was a moment of silence before he spoke again.

"Christian and Lucas had an appointment late last night, they left the estate together but have not yet returned" he muttered.

Now it was her end of the line was silent. Adrian began to panic, after a moment she began to inflict a barrage of questioning. "Where did they go, when were you expecting them back, do you think that something has happened Markus?"

Markus, trying to avoid panicking her any further, chose his response carefully. "They went to meet with Darian, one of the other Clan leaders; we have not heard from them since.

We assume the meeting ran over and they stayed at his estate and should be returning this evening. Don't worry, Ms. Adrian, I'm sure that all is well" he ended.

"Well, I'm not so sure, Christian isn't answering his phone Markus" she replied helplessly.

"Perhaps they are in an area where the phone is not getting a signal, I will have him contact you as soon as I hear from him" Markus added shortly.

Adrian had not been at all comforted by his response.

"Thank you Markus" she mumbled as she ended the call.

Adrian could sense that Markus was not telling her everything, she became consumed with fear over Christian's safety. She strained as she tried to focus on Christian, but could not see nor feel anything. Something had gone terribly wrong and she knew it.

Adrian called the house phone from her cell. "Hello?" Sarah's voice rang.

"Sarah, I need you" Adrian said. Moments later, Adrian could hear the entrance above the suite opening. Sarah rushed into the suite, closing the door tightly behind her. She nervously made her way to Adrian.

"What is it, Ms. Adrian?" she asked in a concerned tone. "I'm sorry I haven't checked on you before, the men are here measuring the windows for your shutters" she explained.

"Very good, when will they be installed?"

"By the end of the week, Miss" Sarah answered.

Adrian nodded in response before informing Sarah of her news. "Sarah, Christian and Lucas did not return to the Estate last night, and I cannot raise Christian on his phone. I am very worried that something has happened to them. I want the contact information for the Grenoble Estate in hopes that I can reach someone there for additional information. I also want for you to pack a suitcase for me and make arrangements for me to go there if something is indeed wrong" she added.

Sarah's face drooped in fear. "I will get the numbers for you immediately, and will have a bag packed for you this evening" Sarah said as she scurried towards the stairwell.

Adrian sat down in Christian's chair in an attempt to calm herself, soon she could hear Sarah returning with the contact information.

"Here you are Ms. Adrian" she said, as she handed over a legal pad containing several numbers. "I am going upstairs to pack for you now" she said as she scurried back to the stairs.

Adrian turned back to the desk and began dialing the first number on the list. "Yes?" the voice of an older man answered.

"To whom am I speaking?" she inquired.

"This is Jeffrey, how may I assist you?" he responded curiously.

"Jeffrey, this is Adrian, Lord Christian's mate, is there a member of the Parliament available for me to speak with?"

"One moment," he replied.

Adrian waited as she stroked the arms of the chair nervously.

"Adrian, how are you?" a woman's voice rang out.

"I'm well, who am I speaking with?" she asked.

"Dear, this is Ruth."

"Oh Ruth! I am so glad that it's you," she exclaimed. "I am worried about Christian and Lucas. Markus told me earlier they had not returned from last night's meeting, and I cannot get Christian to answer his phone" she explained.

Ruth sighed, "I'm afraid that's correct, they have not returned" she stuttered. "We are assuming the meeting ran late and they stayed over" she finished.

Adrian could hear concern in Ruth's voice though she had attempted to hide it.

"Is there any reason we should be worried?" Adrian asked as she fished to see what more Ruth may know.

Ruth hesitated before answering, "Adrian, in these times, it is not recommended any of us let our guard down. I know of no immediate threat but, like you, I would feel much better to see them return" she finished sullenly.

"I wanted to let you know, if we have not heard from them in the next few hours, I am having Sarah make arrangements to get me there."

Ruth laughed, "I know you well enough to say it would do no good to try and discourage you, but are you sure you would be strong enough to travel?" Ruth asked.

"Yes, I fed last night and will feed again tonight so if need be I can leave before dawn to head your way."

"You're feeding already, on your own?" Ruth asked in a surprised tone.

"Yes, I know I am needed right now, and I am hell bent on making a full and speedy recovery" she said.

"Very good Adrian, you are an asset to our race" Ruth stated. "Under the circumstances, I will say I hope to not see you soon" she finished.

Adrian laughed and thanked Ruth for her conversation before ending the call.

Having found no additional information on the whereabouts of Christian, the conversation had not calmed her uneasiness. She sighed and returned the phone to the desk, then decided to lie down and try to rest until sundown. She climbed into her empty bed and curled up around his pillow in search of finding comfort in Christian's scent.

Adrian awoke just before 5:00. She rolled over to check her phone for missed calls or texts from Christian; still nothing. She sighed heavily as she slung the phone back to the nightstand. As the phone began to settle, Adrian was distracted by movement in the stairwell.

Quietly, Sarah opened the door and peeked in to see Adrian standing by the bed with her head in her hands. "Ms. Adrian, if I may ask, have you heard from Christian?" she asked meekly.

Adrian sighed, "No, I haven't, and I am very worried about him."

Sarah paused for a moment, "I'll be right back," she said.

Shortly after, Sarah appeared at the doorway with a glass of wine and a notebook. Adrian turned to face her as the door shut, "Oh, thank you," she said, as she spotted the wine.

Sarah smiled, "I thought you could use it. I have made arrangements for Christian's pilot to take you to Grenoble if need be" she said as she watched Adrian sip at her wine. "He has already left in order to prepare the plane for you, William is prepared drive you if you wish" she finished. Adrian nodded and thanked Sarah for having seen to the details.

Sarah continued to stand quietly before her, wringing her hands anxiously. The moment of uncomfortable silence was soon broken by her nervous announcement, "I am prepared to go with you Miss."

"Oh Sarah, that's not necessary . . ." Adrian began.

"Nonsense, I would have it no other way" Sarah said as she cut off Adrian's words.

Feeling there was no point in arguing, Adrian smiled again and nodded her approval, "Okay" she answered. If there was truly trouble, Sarah would be safest under her watchful eyes.

Sarah turned abruptly and headed to the stairwell. "I have a lot to do, please excuse me Miss," she said as she rushed back up the stairs.

Adrian, now alone, lifted the glass to her lips and sipped at the wine, her mind a whirlwind with thoughts of how she would handle everything that was planned for the evening. She decided to make her way to the vanity and prepare herself for the tasks at hand.

Now dressed, Adrian stood from the vanity as she had completed the final touches of her makeup. As she headed to the stairwell, she decided to try Christian's number one more time before leaving for the evening; still no answer. "If I don't hear from him before I make it back home, I will be leaving for Grenoble tonight" she thought to herself.

Adrian ascended the stairwell and met with Sarah, who had busied herself with cleaning the ceiling fans. "Sarah, I still have not heard from Christian. You should get some rest, because if I do not hear from him before I return, we will be leaving tonight" she announced as she entered the room.

"Yes, Ms. Adrian," Sarah responded as she began to climb down from the step stool. Adrian glanced up just as she missed a step and began to fall. Adrian darted across the room and caught her, slowly lowering her to her feet.

"Oh, thank you Ms. Adrian!" Sarah panted as she shook off the scare.

"No more climbing tonight Sarah," she laughed as she made her way to the door.

"Don't you worry about that" Sarah sighed as she watched Adrian leave.

Adrian smiled as she made her way to the front door. William approached her as she headed to the car. "Good evening, William, I still have not been able to contact Christian, if I do not hear from him before I return, be prepared to drive me to New Orleans this evening" she said as she opened her car door.

"Yes, Ms. Adrian" he responded, as he closed the door behind her. William tapped lightly on her window, "When should I expect your' return?" he asked.

Remembering her promise to him, she rolled the window down to answer, "I shouldn't be gone for more than a few hours, I will text you on my way home," she smiled.

William nodded and stepped away from the car.

Adrian raised the window and sighed heavily as she was now even more burdened by the growing knot in her stomach. She started the car and headed towards the gate, eager to have this evenings' feeding behind her.

Her mind was blank, numbed from worry. She drove blindly to her destination and parked near the front door of the bar. In an attempt to renew her focus on Weston, she scanned the parking lot and saw the same green Buick that she had envisioned earlier. Adrian, now concentrating on the task at hand, killed the motor and walked into the bar.

She immediately saw Weston sitting at the bar involved in an in-depth conversation with the bartender. Adrian walked slowly towards him as she strained to hear their conversation over the blaring jukebox. Unable to determine what was being said, she sat at the bar and placed her drink order. As the bartender turned to fill her order, she turned to Weston and struck up a conversation.

"Nice tattoo," she said as she pointed to his forearm. "Thanks," he answered shortly as he turned to face her. Weston, surprised to find a beautiful woman beside him, smiled as he ogled her. Adrian returned his smile and leaned over the bar, "Bartender, another round for my friend here," she said as she motioned towards Weston.

"Who are you?" Weston asked as he leered at her.

"Apparently no one" she answered sarcastically as she propped her head upon her hand. "I caught my fiancé screwing around on me today," she growled. "I'm going to get very drunk and fuck someone in this bar tonight," she said as she leered back at him.

Weston became immediately aroused, he began to imagine Adrian bound and gagged and at his mercy. He propped himself up on his elbows as he leaned onto the bar. "Might as well be me," he said grinning.

Adrian smiled in return and seductively crossed her legs, "Might as well," she said as she held her glass up to his.

Weston called the bartender over and whispered in his ear. "This deal has to go down now, I'm going to go fuck this chick before I leave town tonight," he boasted.

The bartender looked to Adrian as she downed her drink then nodded as he walked away. Weston leaned over to Adrian, "I'll be right back," he said, as he stood from his stool.

"I'll be right here," she grinned in response.

The two men disappeared into a small room behind the bar, a few minutes they emerged. Weston's demeanor had darkened, he leered eerily into her eyes as he made his way back to her. "Let's blow this joint" he said as he held out his hand to her.

Adrian stood and as she took his hand, she could read his thoughts as his clammy hand touched hers. He intended to rape her, cut her throat and then steal her car.

"Let's see how that works out for you this time," she thought as she grinned to herself. As they exited the bar Adrian turned to him, "Take a ride with me?"

Weston nodded in approval, her offer would make his intentions easier to achieve. They made their way to her car, she unlocked the doors and they both piled in. "I know a quiet little spot about a mile up the road," Adrian said, as she started the car.

"Sounds good to me," Weston said smiling.

Adrian turned up the radio as she made her way onto the highway. She continued to read his thoughts as he plotted her demise, "You're a sick fuck aren't you?" she thought to herself. A few minutes later, she pulled the car onto a rural gravel road and parked inside the tree line. She looked at Weston with a sly grin and said, "On the hood?" Weston nodded enthusiastically.

They exited and met up at the front of the car, their bodies illuminated by the eerie yellow glow of the fog lights below the front bumper. She watched inconspicuously as he pulled something from his waistband. She knew that he would attack once she was within arm's length.

Adrian smiled as they faced each other, "Do you want for me to undress?" she asked as she tugged at her silken shoulder straps.

"Sure!" he replied as he attempted to hide the knife behind his back.

Adrian looked down and pretended that she was about to untie her sash. Weston began to bring his arm around and move towards her. She saw the blade of the knife flash as it caught the light from the full moon above them. Adrian raised her head and looked into his eyes as she bared her fangs at him.

Weston froze in mid-stride as she lunged at him, sinking her fangs into his jugular. His knife dropped to the ground as he struggled hopelessly with her.

She drained him until his heartbeat grew faint. Holding him by the neck with one hand, she lifted him from the ground and leered into his eyes as she spoke. "You were chosen to die tonight. I am here to vindicate the lives of those that you saw fit to take to satisfy your sick urges," she sneered.

Weston hung loosely from her grasp. He gasped for air as his eyes bulged in disbelief of his predicament. Adrian leered at him for a moment longer before she slung him into the nearby tree line. His back cracked as he slammed into a large pine. She slowly walked over to him and stared angrily into his eyes as she snapped his neck for good measure.

Adrian then returned to her car and sat behind the wheel in an attempt to compose herself. His blood pulsed wildly throughout her body, forcing her to witness the grotesque acts that he had subjected upon his victims. She shook the faces of the women and children from her mind and began to focus once more on Christian. Moments later she hurriedly left the scene.

Pulling from the secluded roadway, she reached for her phone to try Christian once more; still no answer. "Damn!" she said aloud as she became overwhelmed with dread. She then immediately texted William to alert him of her return then floored the accelerator and headed for home. She would indeed immediately leave for Christian's New Orleans estate upon her return.

Chapter Four

Adrian pulled into the gate and made her way to the front of the house. William met her at the door in anticipation. "We'll be leaving shortly," she said as she stood from the car.

William nodded in confirmation, "You have still heard nothing from Lord Christian?" he asked in a concerned tone.

Adrian knew that William was consumed with worry. She placed her hand on his shoulder has she approached, "No William, still nothing." She answered solemnly. William nodded once more and lowered his head. Adrian patted his shoulder again before heading towards the door.

She walked into the house and found Sarah sitting eagerly on the couch, her bags sat packed neatly beside her. Sarah diverted her eyes in an attempt not to stare at her blood soaked clothing. "Get ready to leave," Adrian said as she quickly made her way to her suite to change into clean clothes.

She looked into the mirror, shocked by the image that stared back at her. Frantically, she washed her face. As the crimson water flowed into the sink she realized the act she had committed would become an everyday part of life for her. Briefly she succumbed to the remnants of her human emotions and became ill at her realization. "Fuck!" she exclaimed as she began to remove her clothes in anticipation of a quick shower.

For one brief moment she felt a hint of remorse as she watched the last of the fiends' blood wash away down the drain. She sighed as she reminded herself how she had selected her prey, now sated in knowing she had made the right choice.

Now feeling a bit less tainted, she made her way into the bedroom and dressed before heading back to the main level, closing the entrance to the suite behind her as she left.

Upon entering the living room she found Sarah and William loading the last of their luggage into the limo. William ushered them into the back of the car and shortly after they began to roll towards the gate.

Within the hour they were pulling into the main gate of Christian's New Orleans estate, down the long tree lined drive and through the back of the property to the hangar. The pilot stood next to the steps, which were lowered and awaiting them.

William stopped the car next to the cargo hold where he and the pilot would begin loading their luggage as Adrian and Sarah boarded the plane. Adrian saw the limo pull into the hanger shortly after. Within a few minutes, the jet was making its way down the runway.

The pilot announced, "We will be taking off momentarily."

Adrian fell back into the leather sofa where she had sat next to Christian on their last flight in from Grenoble. She ran her hand over the cushion and sighed as she tried to imagine him there. "Sarah, I want for you to contact the estate and let them know that I am on my way. Ask if they have heard anything." She curled up onto the couch and looked out of the window to take in the New Orleans skyline as they gained altitude.

"Yes Ms. Adrian." Sarah replied as she made her way to the cockpit. Sarah returned shortly with her report. "I spoke with Naomi and told her that we were on our way. They still have had no word from Lucas or Christian, I'm sorry," she said as she sat on the couch next to her.

Adrian's eyes filled with tears, she knew Christian was in trouble. She tried desperately to focus on him and became even more frustrated as she was too emotional to sense anything.

Sarah tried hopelessly to comfort her, eventually she stood from the couch and made her way to the bar to pour herself and Adrian each a glass of wine.

Adrian gratefully accepted the glass and then returned her gaze out of the window into the night sky.

A few hours later Adrian awoke still curled up on the couch. The pilot was announcing their final descent. She looked around the cabin and saw that the shutters had all been lowered. There across from her lay Sarah sound asleep. "She must be exhausted, this has surly taken its toll on her." Adrian thought.

She stood and stretched, then gathered the empty wine glasses and took them to the sink behind the bar. With nothing left to do but wait, she lit a cigarette and returned to her seat until landing. Within a few minutes she could hear the tires screaming as they hit the runway.

Shortly after the plane was nestled inside of the hanger. William entered the cabin, "Miss Adrian, the sun has not yet set, I will go to the estate to consult with the security staff," he said solemnly. "I will hurry back and brief you on what I have learned," he said as he fought his muscular frame into a navy blue blazer.

Adrian nodded in confirmation as she anxiously wrung her hands.

With nearly two hours until nightfall, Adrian paced the cabin relentlessly. She, knowing that her attempts were futile, retrieved her cellphone and tried to call Christian again; her call went straight to voice mail. "His battery is dead," she thought to herself. Suddenly she caught a glimpse of his phone in his hand and could see her number was the last number he had tried to call. She could see that he was lying in a dark and confined space and then the vision disappeared as quickly as it had come.

"He's in a coffin!" she blurted out suddenly, causing Sarah to jump in shock. "Oh God, he's in a coffin somewhere and I think he's buried!" Adrian shrieked as she collapsed onto the couch. Sarah ran to her and tried to comfort her. "I can't see him anymore" she wailed.

"Dear, he's probably sleeping and should be awake here in just a little while, as soon as the sun sets," Sarah said as she placed her hand on Adrian's shoulder.

"He is not asleep, he is in trouble, he knows it and now I know it!" Adrian shouted frantically.

She saw turmoil all about him. She saw his eyes were closed but sensed he was not asleep, he was completely unaware . . . it was as if he were in some form of hibernation. She could also sense that he was very weak; he was in trouble indeed. As she focused on him, there were no thoughts in his mind; she could read absolutely nothing from him, which had nearly threw her into a desperate and frantic state.

Adrian stood and began to pace anxiously once more; she lit a cigarette just as William entered the cabin. "There is not much to report, Ms. Adrian," he said, as he hung his head. "Security tells me only that he and Lucas had a meeting arranged and left the Estate at approximately eight o'clock that night." he said warily adding . . . "No one has heard from either of them since."

"Who drove them? Where is the driver and the car?" she asked, as she desperately tried to sort through details.

He hung his head as he knew that his response would further upset her, "The driver has not returned and there is no sign of the car." He answered while looking up at her briefly.

Adrian flung herself onto the couch and tried to clear her mind, as she would need to be able to focus in order to be of any help to Christian and Lucas. "What time is it now?" she asked as she turned to Sarah. "Sunset's in twenty minutes, Ms. Adrian." Sarah answered.

Adrian took a deep breath and began to plan what she would do first upon leaving the plane. "I need to go to Christian's suite first," she thought aloud. "I need something that belongs to the driver" she continued to mumble as she made her mental checklist.

Adrian was deep in thought but was inadvertently issuing orders to Sarah and William who immediately reacted as she listed her needs. Sarah had already lifted the in-cabin phone and was making arrangements when Adrian turned to make her request. "Sarah contact the staff inside of the estate…" she began. Her voice trailed off as she realized Sarah was already speaking with someone in her behalf.

She stopped in her tracks as she realized William and Sarah were just as upset as she was, they needed for her to be focused. They too loved Christian and were worried sick, "I need to calm down, for Christian's sake as well as theirs, surely they feel even more helpless than I," she thought to herself.

After having taken a deep breath Adrian walked over next to Sarah. "Will you let them know I will need access to Lucas' study as well," she requested calmly.

Sarah glanced over and nodded in confirmation as she moved the handset away from her mouth, "Ruth and Naomi both want to accompany you this evening." Sarah whispered.

Adrian nodded slowly, "Ask them if they will follow us. I'm afraid they will inadvertently be a distraction to me once I have started to search for him," she mumbled calmly.

Sarah turned her head and repeated the request to Ruth, then turned back to Adrian. "They understand," she said. Sarah briefly turned her attention back to the conversation, "Miss Adrian will need access to Lucas' study." After a brief moment of silence she turned to nod their confirmation to Adrian as then returned the phone back to its receiver.

Now that the call had ended, William turned to exit the cabin. "I will come get you as soon as the sun has set Ms. Adrian," he said as he walked down the steps.

Adrian was in returned to her deep train of thought by then and did not respond. She tried desperately to focus on Christian leaving the estate that night, but she saw nothing. Frustrated, she drew her hands to her head and slouched back onto the couch. Shortly after she could hear the hangar doors sliding open.

William appeared in the doorway "Ms. Adrian, it is time to go," he said warmly as he held his hand out for her.

Adrian looked into his eyes and smiled as she stood. They proceeded to the steps together, she taking William's hand as a gesture of trust in him. "You should close your eyes as we exit, it is not completely dark yet," he cautioned. "We will need to move to the car quickly to avoid causing you any discomfort" he added as they descended the steps.

Adrian closed her eyes and walked quickly with William toward the car. She could feel the last of the sun's dimming rays begin to burn her skin. A sharp pain began to pulse throughout her body; a wave of nausea hit her just as they were seated into the car. William threw his jacket over her and quickly shut the door.

Seconds later he joined her in the car, "I'm sorry Ms. Adrian but I knew you were in a hurry to get started," he said as he signaled the driver to proceed.

"It's okay, I am in a hurry" she said as she fought back the urge to vomit.

The car rolled to a stop shortly after, just as she was beginning to settle. William swung the car door open and ushered her into the Estate, his jacket still draped over her head.

The heavy steel doors closed behind them and William removed his jacket. Adrian strained to focus her eyes then began to move forward, up the stairs and to Christian's suite.

She slowly walked into the door scanning the room for any sense of where he may be. The room was just as it had been when they last had been there together. She looked at the massive bed and remembered their passionate lovemaking, his beautiful face etched in ecstasy. She pushed back her thoughts in order to focus on Christian's last night in the room.

She wandered about, touching things that he would have recently touched; she made her way to the bathroom and stood frozen in front of the mirror. She stared intently into her own eyes and found that she could see Christian moving about the room dressing himself in preparation for the meeting in Milan.

"He was going to Milan" she announced.

"Yes, Milan," she heard, a familiar voice repeating her words.

Adrian's gaze, now broken, was turned to the doorway to see Naomi and Ruth standing. Ruth approached her, "I am sorry I disturbed you," she said. "Christian and Lucas were going to Milan in order to have their meeting with Darian," she ended.

"Hi Naomi, Ruth" Adrian said as she acknowledged their presence. "So who is Darian?" she prodded.

It was Naomi that responded, "Darian was a member of the Parliament centuries ago, he is an ally, he is also an introvert" she answered.

"Let's give Darian a call, shall we?" Adrian said as she made her way out of the suite, "I would like to see how he responds when he is asked about the whereabouts of Christian and Lucas" she finished.

Adrian led the way down the long staircase, Ruth, Naomi, Sarah and William in tow.

Ruth caught up to her. "You said you needed access to Lucas' study, we will make the call from there," she said as she now took the lead. As they reached the door Adrian stopped Ruth.

"Perhaps I can walk through the study alone briefly to see if there is anything there for me to pick up on; if there are other people in the room I may be distracted," she said.

Ruth nodded her head in approval and opened the door.

Adrian proceeded into the study while the others waited for her in the hall. She wandered about the dimly lit room and was drawn to Lucas' desk.

There in front of her lay a world map with several red X's noting that one of them marked her home in southern Louisiana. She realized the marks represented attacks. Seven in all, she now knew that Daphne's demise had not ended anything. She thought back to the other clan leaders that she had implicated when the plot had been discovered.

Adrian ran her hands across the map and then walked behind the desk to sit and focus on it as Lucas had. As her eyes landed on one of the marks to the West she began to see glimpses of an attack. She recognized the twins, Daphne's cohorts, along with the Clan Leader whom she had referred to as "the tip of the spear" previously, but now she knew as Lazigne.

"It seems Lazigne is still not aware of the journal Daphne kept," she announced as she turned to look at Naomi. "Who did you deliver the journal to?" she demanded.

"I left it with the twins," she growled. "Aramond promised me he would personally deliver it to Lazigne," she spat.

"It seems to me the twins have now taken on Daphne's plot," Adrian said as she returned her gaze to the map. Blankly, she continued to stare, to no avail; no new information on the whereabouts of Christian or Lucas were revealed. "Shall we make that call to Darian now?" she asked as she lifted her eyes from the desk.

Ruth made her way to the desk and lifted the phone as she dialed. "Good evening, Darian," she said as she looked to Adrian. "I am well, I have a question to ask of you," she continued. "I understand that Lucas and Christian had made arrangements to meet with you two nights ago, what happened?" she asked politely.

Adrian looked up immediately and answered for him, "They never made it there."

Ruth looked to her and nodded her head, confirming Adrian was correct.

As Ruth continued to speak with Darian, Adrian began to catch glimpses of what had happened. She could see them sitting in the back of the car consumed by deep conversation, suddenly there was a loud thud on the roof. The driver slammed on brakes and the car slid sideways stopping in the middle of the deserted country road. Immediately they were surrounded by several black vehicles, which skidded towards them from all directions. She saw Christian exit the car and then the scene went black.

Ruth was ending her call as the vision faded from her grasp. "He was very worried about them" she began. "He had been expecting them all night and they never showed up or called," Ruth finished as she sighed.

"I know," Adrian said as she turned to face her. "Were you able to find anything that belonged to the driver?" she asked.

"I thought that I would take you to his quarters on our way out," she replied.

Adrian nodded and turned to William, "Bring a car around front I'm ready to leave now, there is little time to spare," she finished as she stood from the desk.

"Where are we going?" Naomi asked.

"We are going to find the scene of the attack, I believe that the car is still there," Adrian announced, as she made her way out of the office and towards the grand entrance.

Naomi and Ruth sped to follow her. "Attack? You said attack, what is it that you saw?" Ruth asked nervously as they rushed through the foyer.

"Not enough," she answered testily.

Naomi reached over and grabbed Ruth's arm just as she was about to respond to Adrian. "This is why we have to follow her, stop with the constant disruptions!" she scolded.

"You're right" she whispered as they closed in behind Adrian. They were both uncertain of her intentions yet were eager to assist in any way possible; even if that meant to follow along and hold their silence.

Adrian stepped out onto the curb just as two black limos pulled up to the entrance, one for her and William the other for Ruth and Naomi.

Naomi instructed the first driver to stop off at the living quarters before they left the estate then proceeded to her car.

Just to the right of the wrought iron entrance was a small drive that she had not noticed before. The drive went back about seventy-five feet to reveal several small cottage-style homes. The limo was now coming to a stop in front of the third cottage. Adrian opened the car door and approached the front porch, hesitating for a deep breath before she opened the door. Once inside the small but well-kept residence, she realized there was no point in looking any further.

"He's dead," she mumbled. "He's in the trunk of the car," she added as she walked back out of the cottage.

The others had barely made it out of the cars as Adrian was on her way back. She announced to them what she had seen and climbed back into the limo.

William had never experienced Adrian in this state. He was concerned with the blank expression upon her face; he grew anxious as he looked into her glazed eyes and received no response from her. "Are you alright Ms. Adrian?" he pried.

Adrian, having been distracted again, realized William only wanted to help. She would have to instruct him as to how she worked when she was in a trance.

"I'm fine, thank you William," she answered. "William, I am going to tell you which direction to drive," she began. "It will appear I'm in some trance like state, it is important I am not disturbed by anyone other than you while I'm like this. It is okay if you need to ask a question, but only you," she added. "Instruct the driver that he must not speak, nor can I be disturbed in any other way; this includes a phone ringing," she said as she retrieved her own phone to mute the volume.

William nodded as he nervously fumbled for his phone and muted it as well. "I understand" he responded as he turned off the driver's microphone. "Can you hear me?" he asked as he plugged an earphone into his left ear.

The driver nodded in response.

"Miss Adrian will be giving me directions but cannot be disturbed, I have turned off your microphone," William informed him. "You will only be communicating with me, and that must be kept to a minimum; do you understand?" William asked.

The driver nodded his head once more in confirmation as he shifted the car into gear. "We're all set," William said as he turned to Adrian.

"Thanks William, here we go," she smiled warmly.

Chapter Five

Adrian began to focus intensely on the roadway before them. William watched warily as her eyes shifted hue. He found her eyes fierce and draining; he realized that he would have to avoid eye contact with her if he were to be of any assistance.

After a moment of silence, Adrian raised her hand and pointed to the right.

William relayed her directions to the driver and the car began to move forward.

They drove for forty-two minutes in silence before Adrian lifted her hand and pointed to the right once more.

William relayed her directions to the driver once more.

They traveled for another twenty minutes before Adrian gasped loudly, throwing her hands into the air while shouting "Here! Stop right here!"

The car slid to an abrupt stop, slamming both she and William back into their seats. The driver had stopped the car in the center of the road and turned on the high beams in order to better light the scene.

Still under the influence of her vision, she exited the car and stood in the middle of the highway. Adrian began to walk forward with the car slowly following her as she progressed. She continued for several more yards before she stopped and fell to her knees.

Her eyes slowly cleared as she faced the pavement, there beneath her were tire tracks, blood and glass. She became dizzied by the realization that the worst of her fears had been true, Adrian knew that she had found the scene where something horrible had happened to Christian.

William rushed to her side and reached for her. Adrian fought to recapture her trance in order to gather more information. She was distracted again momentarily; she could hear Naomi in the background as she sped to stop William.

"Don't touch her while she is in this state!" she hissed as she snatched his arm away.

Adrian knelt down and placed her palms onto the cool, damp pavement. Flashes of the attack began to pulse through her. She began to hiss in anger as the scenes played on, subjecting her to the same pain and frustration that Christian and Lucas had experienced on that night.

The others stood quietly as they watched on. They knew Adrian was suffering, each of them helpless in assisting her. The expressions on her face made her appear as though she were observing the attack in its entirety. Suddenly, her head jolted to the right.

Adrian stood and began walking towards the thick woods that surrounded the old highway. She had seen it in her vision; the car had been driven into the thicket by 2 of the masked men in black. It was indeed well hidden from view as the men had placed broken tree limbs all about in order to hide the tracks.

She tore through the thicket, immediately unveiling the car to the others who were only steps behind her now. Adrian walked to the right rear door and touched it, as it was the last thing she knew that Christian had touched. She could feel his shock and rage; he knew that there was no point in trying to fight them off, there were too many of them. She felt the anger boil within him as he watched Lucas be thrown to the ground and chained like a beast. Her heart sank, partly over the torment of having to witness the attack and partly due to her absorption of Christian's emotions as he reacted to their dilemma.

She tried to look through his eyes to see if he had any idea who the attackers were. She sensed that some were mortal but most were Vampire. She watched on as Christian and Lucas were surrounded. Suddenly, Lazigne and the twins emerged from the darkness. Christian was furious as he now who had been responsible for the attack that had mortally wounded her and had taken the lives of so many others in the past few months.

Christian attempted to fight them off as they bound him in the same silver chains that Lucas wore. She could hear his skin burning and began to feel the pain as he himself had experienced it. Adrian struggled to hold on to the vision but the level of pain was becoming unbearable. She struggled to watch on until Christian and Lucas were both loaded into the back of a black van, never taking her eyes off of it until the tail lights faded into nothing.

Adrian lay writhing on the ground until she had shaken the grasp of the trance. Slowly she began to regain her composure. Ruth and Naomi rushed to her side as her eyes cleared. With their assistance, she stood just in time to see William open the trunk to reveal the body of the driver, just as she had said.

She, Ruth and Naomi slowly made their way to the rear of the car and glanced down into the trunk to see the mangled and blood-soaked remains of the driver; his face frozen in a horrified yet silent scream.

Adrian reached up and closed the trunk, "There is nothing that we can do for him now," she mumbled as she looked at them. "We must be leaving," she said as she turned to make her way back to the car.

William obediently followed her as did the others and soon they were moving forward down the desolate and darkened highway.

Adrian's eyes glazed over once more; she began to see the van's tail lights in the distance. Only a few miles from the scene of the attack, the van slowed then veered off of the highway and to the right, vanishing within the thick woods.

Adrian began to feel a pressure building within her; she now knew that Christian and Lucas were nearby. Abruptly she flung her hand and pointed, startling William with her sudden movement. William immediately instructed the driver to stop.

The moonlight only hinted at a secluded and beaten dirt road that was hidden within the dense overgrowth. William motioned for the driver to proceed as Adrian sat staring intensely ahead as if she was focusing on what lay at the end of the road.

Slowly the cars made their way through the obscuring over-growth and onto the rugged roadway and up the hillside, where the sky seemed to open. There below lay the remnants of an old abandoned mining facility.

The car stopped at a fork in the road. Adrian reached for the door handle and stood from the car. Still under the influence of her trance, she walked ahead to the front of the car and began to scan the openings in the mountainsides across the massive pits from where they now stood. It was as if she were looking into the Grand Canyon. The hillside was immense and dotted with openings. The cold night wind howled through the caverns as she stood and silently scanned the terrain from east to west. Suddenly, her gaze was drawn to an opening a hundred yards east of where she stood. Without a word, she frantically began to run towards the opening.

William chased behind her shouting, "Adrian, get in the car!" She froze in her steps as the car pulled up beside her. Adrian, too preoccupied to argue, slid into the back seat and pointed towards the opening as she tried desperately to make contact with Christian. She sat upon the edge of the seat and focused through the windshield as she called out to him. Everything within her told her that he was there but she could not reach him, nor could she see him.

The car crept slowly through the rugged terrain. William whispered into his microphone, "Keep an eye out for fresh tire tracks." William noticed that Adrian was growing extremely agitated as they approached. Before the car was able to stop, she leapt from the now opened door and ran up the steep pass and into the cavern leaving the others scurrying behind her to catch up.

Now convinced that they were in the right place, Adrian desperately called out for him but to no avail. She stood quietly and began to panic as she stared towards a set of three openings before her. Ruth and Naomi appeared beside her as she scanned her surroundings for some clue of Christian and Lucas' position. "I don't know where to go now," she moaned frantically as she continued to stare forward.

Ruth stepped forward and in an attempt to steady her, placed her hands on Adrian's shoulders. "Adrian, between the three of us we can search the caverns quickly, what are we looking for?" she asked.

"I'm not certain of that either, but I know that they are here," she replied. "I want to take that one," she said as she motioned to the far-right opening.

Naomi nodded as she looked to Ruth and pointed to the center opening. Within a moment all three of them had vanished into the darkness of the tunnels leaving William behind as he had just reached the openings.

Adrian ran through the tunnel frantically searching for any sign of recent activity. Several yards into the darkness, she began to sense the presence of someone else ahead of her. The scent was obviously human, the faint echo of their heartbeats confirming their mortality. She stopped and crouched down against the wall for a moment before she began to cautiously proceed. She called out to Ruth and Naomi in hopes that they would hear her the way that she and Christian could hear each other.

As Adrian was a new Vampire, she did not know if it would work on all Vampires, or if it worked only between her and Christian, as he had turned her. "If you can hear me, I think I'm in the right place and I am not alone," she thought.

Slowly, she crept down the narrowing passage until a dim light began to appear ahead. Suddenly, she was startled as she felt Ruth and Naomi appear behind her. The surge of adrenaline now subsiding, she acknowledged them, "I'm glad you heard me," she whispered over her shoulder. "The humans may not be here alone."

The three of them now crept slowly and quietly towards the light. Adrian was the first to spot two armed guards sitting opposite each other at an opening. She looked back to Naomi; nodding simultaneously they pounced onto the unsuspecting guards. The men having no warning and little time to struggle were quickly drained; their limp bodies now fell to the ground. Naomi smiled as she looked into Adrian's face, "You have adapted quickly," she whispered. Adrian grinned as she leaned over and snapped the neck of her victim for good measure. "I am angry, I only regret that I cannot kill him twice," she sneered as she looked back at Naomi.

The three of them proceeded cautiously, and found that the tiny dank opening would soon end at a huge cavern.

The walls were lined with smaller openings as high as the eye could see; it was immense. The three of them stood back-to-back and examined the hive-like openings, a feeling of hopelessness now washed over them. Adrian began to try to contact Christian again as Ruth and Naomi did with Lucas. She closed her eyes. "I am here for you, just a little help Christian, where are you?" She strained to filter through the memories of the human that she had just encountered. She was becoming frustrated as the humans' memories only confirmed that Christian indeed was inside one of the caverns, but she could not determine which one.

She forced herself to focus harder then, suddenly she began to feel as if she were being pulled through a small dark tunnel. Adrian opened her eyes and found herself staring to an opening just above her. Without hesitation she sped up the ledge and to the opening to find herself facing a pile of freshly-moved rocks.

Adrian began to claw viciously at the large stones until eventually she was able to run her arm through to the other side. Fueled by her progress she began to dig more furiously until she was able to fit through. There in the small, dark cell was a wooden coffin wrapped in silver chains with a large pad lock connecting them. "Dear God, what have they done to you?" she gasped as she shuddered in anger at the sight before her.

Desperately searching for a way to release him, she reached for a nearby rock and began to pound on the padlock, breaking it with her second blow. She clawed the lid of the coffin away to see what was left of her Christian wrapped in chains and burned beyond recognition. Though he lay motionless and silent, she could sense his presence and knew he had not left his body.

Adrian snatched and pulled at the chains, her skin burning from the contact but in her frenzied rage to free Christian, she felt nothing. Soon she had freed him of the chains and was pulling him from the coffin. She lay on the stone floor with him on top of her, searching his scorched face for some sign of life.

She gently flipped them over and bit her wrist open to feed him, as he had done for her. "Feed Christian, please, feed!" she cried out as blood trickled from her wound and into what remained of his mouth. Suddenly she heard scurrying about her. She lifted her head to see Naomi and Ruth now inside the cell with her. "What of Lucas?" she asked the two.

"Lucas is in the same condition that your Christian is in. The drivers are moving him to the car already. We are here to help you with Christian." Naomi said.

"Sunrise will be approaching soon, we need to leave here immediately" Ruth added as they knelt beside her.

Adrian nodded in confirmation and looked down into Christian's face, desperate for any response; still none. "Will he be okay?" she asked, as she looked up into Ruth's face.

"We will do everything possible, but for now we need to get him out of here," she replied.

Naomi approached the opening and began to claw at the rocks, moving them so they could get Christian out of the cell. Adrian and Ruth both joined in and moments later they were rushing Christian out and towards the car.

William saw them emerging from the caverns and opened the rear car door for them. Adrian entered first and slid to the end so that she could hold Christian's head in her lap. She glanced over at Lucas, who most certainly was in the same condition. She could see by the blood on his charred face where Naomi and Ruth had both tried to feed him as well.

Naomi sat at Christian's feet, while Ruth entered from the other side of the car in order to hold Lucas' head in her lap.

Chapter Six

The car began to roll its' way cautiously back to the highway. Once on pavement, the driver sped back to the estate. As they approached the gate, Ruth lowered her window and motioned for the guard.

"We need all donors gathered inside of the estate immediately." The guard glanced down and saw the condition of the two Lords and immediately radioed his orders as he watched the car speed towards the main entrance.

The staff spilled out of the doors before the car slid to a full stop. Lucas and Christian were transported from the car while the guards ushered Ruth, Naomi and Adrian from beneath the now graying sky and into the estate. The doors and shutters slammed closed behind them they entered the foyer.

The scene was a methodic symphony of organized chaos. Everything was moving so fast around them that Adrian was being pushed away from Christian by the staff as they frantically fed needles into him.

Overwhelmed and exhausted she stood motionlessly as she numbly watched the guards scurry by while members of the staff shouted orders back and forth. Now with evidence that the Lords had undergone an attack, the security forces would be doubling. Team leaders were already being gathered in the west wing of the estate, eager to be briefed by William.

Lucas and Christian were brought into a makeshift recovery room in the lower level of the estate. Adrian followed the crowd inside the room to see guards seating on either side of Christian and Lucas, rolling up their sleeves in order to have IV's inserted. More stools were being brought in by the staff and placed along the sides of the bed as a line of eager donors continued to gather about the room.

Adrian stood quietly in the background, astonished by the level of loyalty that his men displayed. She sensed that they felt it to be a great honor to assist Christian and Lucas in their time of need. These were loyal mortals, loyal to Lucas and her Christian!

Ruth came to stand by Adrian, who was tattered and exhausted. "There's not much that can be done now but wait."

"I will not leave him," Adrian responded. "He did not leave me" she muttered as she stood staring blankly towards him."

Ruth nodded in understanding and placed her hand upon Adrian's shoulder before turning to leave.

Once all of the Guards were seated and IV's run, Adrian crossed the room and stood behind Christian, placing her hands on either side of his head. His skin crumbled at her touch; her eyes filled with tears as she began to speak to him through her thoughts.

"Christian, please come back to me, you have to fight, I need you, and I will not lose you!" Tears streamed down her filthy face, she felt no response at all from him.

Adrian stood by him unflinching for hours. Elizabeth approached and placed her hand lightly on her forearm. "Please, Ms. Adrian, sit," she said timidly as she moved a stool behind her.

Adrian lifted her head, "Thank you," she said weakly as she laid her head next to his and wrapped her arms across his brittle chest. Exhausted both physically and mentally, sleep soon crept upon her.

Sometime just before sunset, Adrian was awakened by movement beneath her. She slowly lifted her head to see Christian moving his hand towards hers. "Christian!" She cried as she jumped up to face him.

Christian slowly opened his deep dark eyes and fought to focus on Adrian's beautiful face. "Oh, Christian!" she cried out as she wrapped her arms gently around him and held him.

"You came for me" he managed to grunt.

"Yes, Christian, I came, of course I came" she cried.

The staff, noticing the commotion, rushed to his side. The line of new donors were readying themselves for IV's and the room had erupted in chatter as Lord Christian had awoken! He tried to lift his head as the commotion around him startled him.

"Lie still," Adrian ordered. "We are back at the Grenoble estate." Everything is fine," she said, as she stroked the charred flesh from his slowly healing face.

Christian lowered his head back to the pillow and continued to stare into Adrian's eyes. She could hear his thoughts: "How long have we been here?" he asked.

"Since just before dawn this morning, a few hours." You should rest now," she responded to him silently.

Christian obediently closed his eyes, "Thank you," he said as he surrendered to sleep.

Adrian pulled her stool closer beside him and wrapped her hand around his. She lay her head on the bed next to him and soon found sleep of her own.

Not long after she was awakened again by more commotion within the room. Lucas himself had awakened. The staff surrounded his bed as they tended to him. She watched them intently as they shuffled about him.

She looked down at Christian who was now beginning to stir himself. Adrian leaned over and whispered in his ear. "Lucas is awake," she said as she stroked his nearly healed face. Only a few small red blotches remained, far from the scalded and peeling skin had covered his body before.

Christian slowly began to open his beautiful dark eyes to see Adrian hovering above him. "You are so beautiful," he whispered to her.

"How are you feeling now?" she asked, as she brushed his hair from his face.

"Much better," he said, smiling.

Christian began to sit up in the bed; Adrian placed her arm behind his back to help him. She giggled as he sat. "How would you feel about a hot bath?" she asked, as he had asked her the same upon her recovery.

Christian looked up at her and nodded, to which she replied, "Thank God, because you smell horrible!" He looked to her and smiled more broadly as she continued to laugh.

She motioned for Elizabeth and began to instruct her, "I want you to prepare a bath and fresh clothes for Christian in our suite. Arrange for the guards to help me relocate him, as we will want our privacy." Elizabeth nodded in confirmation and scurried away to complete her tasks.

"Have the guards help me over to Lucas, I want to see him before we go upstairs," Christian said weakly. No sooner had the words left his lips than the guards approached him. Christian slowly stood as they carried him carefully across the room.

Christian hovered over Lucas as his eyes slowly opened. "Glad to see you, my old friend" Christian smiled. Lucas mumbled incoherently before closing his eyes again.

Relieved Lucas had awakened, Christian was now content to leave him with the staff. "It will take him longer to recover," he said weakly as he turned to Adrian.

"It will take a while for you to recover as well and I intend to see to it," Adrian smiled. She turned to the guards and nodded, signaling for them to take Christian upstairs to his suite.

The guards lifted him upon their shoulders and carried him up the wide staircase and into his quarters, Adrian followed closely behind.

"Please seat him in the chair near the bathtub," she instructed them. They carefully lowered Christian into the high backed chair and turned to her for further direction. "That will be all, thank you so much for all of your loyalty to us in our time of need, it will not be forgotten," she said as she bowed her head slightly.

"Yes Mistress," they replied before exiting the room.

Elizabeth had just finished drawing his bath and placing clean clothes for him onto the vanity. Adrian dismissed her as well upon her finishing her tasks. With the suite having emptied she walked over to Christian who had already begun attempting to remove the scorched and tattered clothing from his body. "I don't think so," she said smiling at him.

Christian looked up at her with a baffled expression upon his face. Adrian smiled as she now stood in front of him and began to undress him. "I am taking care of you just as you took care of me," she said as she pulled the filthy rags from his body.

She could still see where the chains had burned through his skin across his chest. The smile she had worn since he awoke had now faded from her face. She fell to her knees in knowing the pain he had felt. Placing her head upon his chest, she began to cry.

"I nearly lost you," she sobbed. Christian draped his arms around her neck and held her; she raised from him and sniffed back her tears. "I will slaughter every Vampire and human that had anything to do with this! I will rip them open and stake them to the ground to greet the rising sun!" she growled. "They are lucky I am distracted with your recovery at the moment, else I would be hunting them down right now!" she added.

Christian smiled a broad smile at her vengeful declarations.

She continued disrobing him as he sat submissively. She had finally removed the last of the burned rags from his body and was now helping him stand so that she could get him into the tub.

Within moments Christian lay in the steaming water. Adrian sat behind him and began to bathe him. Lovingly, she labored at removing the burned and scaling skin from him while he sat quietly.

"What are you thinking?" Adrian asked, as she was too drained to read his thoughts.

"I am thinking how lucky I am to have you, as well as plotting my revenge on those that have caused us so much pain," he answered.

She smiled and nodded as she sat next to him on the ledge of the tub. "I understand; however, let's focus all of our energy on you healing for the moment," she finished. "The time will soon come for our revenge" she added.

Adrian drew her wrist to her mouth and opened it widely for him. "Feed," she said, as she offered her arm to him.

Christian shook his head and turned away from her wound. "You are too weak, you need to feed, I will not take blood from you" he responded. "This is another argument that you will not win, Christian," she said, as she placed her wrist against his mouth. Begrudgingly he began to drink from her opened wound.

Adrian found herself wildly aroused as he fed from her. She sighed heavily as he removed her wrist from his mouth. Christian kissed her lightly on her hand as he rinsed the blood from her, just as she had done for her in her recovery.

She watched as his scars began to fade, lifting her hand to touch his skin as he healed. "Let's get you dressed and back to bed," she said as she stood. "I want to go and visit with Lucas again" he said as he stood.

"Another argument that you will not win," she stated adamantly as she wrapped him with a nearby towel.

He rolled his eyes and smirked as she dried his still scarred body. Her mind was made up, he knew that any argument from him would only result in wasted energy.

Adrian sensing his disappointment looked into his eyes as she stood, "We will call downstairs and check on him once I have you in bed," she smiled in response to his reaction.

Adrian wrapped her arm around his waist, steadying him as they made their way across the room and into the bed. Once he had settled she retrieved the phone from the bedside table and dialed downstairs to check on the condition of Lucas.

"He is awake now and feeding" she reported. Christian reached for the phone, Adrian hesitated momentarily before surrendering it to him.

"Send two donors to my suite, one for me and one for Ms. Adrian" he said.

Adrian immediately protested.

Christian smirked as he ended the call. He handed her the phone and looked deeply into her eyes, "How can you continue to protect me in your weakened state?" He knew full well his statement would strike a nerve; these were the same words that she had used to encourage him to feed from her. She stood quietly and at a loss for words, she knew that she had no response.

"An argument you will not win today my Adrian," Christian said weakly as he looked up at her grinning. He was quite pleased with himself for having won one round with her at this point.

"Augh!" she exclaimed as she noted the grin on his face, "I cannot believe that you just stooped to that level," she said.

"Nonetheless, I win," he said still gloating. Suddenly there was a knock at the door. "Enter" he tolled, still smiling broadly.

The door opened and in rushed Sarah escorting two guards inside the room and to Christians' bedside. The guards had already inserted IV's and were ready to donate their blood.

Adrian looked up to see that one of the guards was approaching her. She peered deeply into his eyes as he knelt before her to insert the needle into her arm. Sensing no ill will on his part she held her arm out toward him.

"I'm sorry about this but Christian insisted," she apologized.

The guard seemed shocked by her response. "No, Ms. Adrian, this is an honor for me," he responded.

Once again Adrian sat quietly, amazed by the reverence displayed by the guard. The awkward silence was broken as Sarah approached.

"You should lie down," she coaxed as she inserted the needle.

Adrian followed Sarah's instruction and lay on the bed next to Christian, who reached for her hand as she settled. The guards sat patiently as their blood was being transferred. A short while later Sarah had removed the needles and was escorting the guards from the room.

"Will you be needing anything else?" she asked before closing the door.

"No, Sarah, thank you for seeing over us," Adrian said warmly.

"It has been an honor," Sarah responded as she backed away and closed the door softly behind herself.

Adrian felt her strength beginning to return but was still mentally exhausted; she rolled over to look into Christian's eyes and found he was fast asleep. She draped her arm over his chest and moved closer to him, so happy to be beside him once more. Anger began to build within her as she stared at the still faintly visible scars across his chest. She wrapped her arms around him and held him tightly to her.

You mother fuckers will regret this in the worst of ways, she vowed silently as she closed her eyes to rest.

Chapter Seven

Adrian woke refreshed, she rolled over to look at Christian but found she was alone. "Oh, no, he didn't!" she exclaimed as she sat up in the bed. She reached for her phone to check the time; she had slept for over twelve hours, dusk would soon arrive. She knew it would be difficult to keep Christian confined within the walls of the estate once darkness fell. Adrian sighed heavily as she swung her legs over the side of the bed, "I best prepare myself for a long night," she thought aloud as she stood.

Knowing full well Christian had gone to be with Lucas, Adrian began to draw a bath. As she began to undress she could hear the door open.

"Ms. Adrian?" Sarah tolled.

"I'm here, Sarah, in the bathroom," she said as she stepped into the tub.

Sarah made her way around the corner. "I came to check in on you. I've brought you some wine. Is there anything that I can do to help you?" she asked as she approached.

"Sarah, you are too good to me," Adrian responded as she accepted the glass from her. "Is Christian with Lucas?" she asked as she raised the glass to her lips.

"Yes, Ms. Adrian." Sarah responded, as she made her way to the bed to strip the linens.

"How is he?" she asked.

"Lucas is doing much better, his wounds are healing and he is coherent," Sarah responded, as she stripped the soiled cases from the pillows.

"I am very happy to hear that," she said as she rinsed the soap from her body. "I will go see him as soon as I am presentable," she said.

Sarah nodded as she made her way to Adrian, her arms laden with the linens from their bed. "If there is nothing else, Ms. Adrian?" she said as she waited for a response.

"No, Sarah, thank you again for everything." Adrian smiled.

Sarah returned her smile, bowing her head slightly before turning for the door.

Adrian sank back into the deep tub and relaxed as she finished her glass of wine. Her mind was quiet, her body relaxed; yet in the inner stillness Adrian began to feel a knot of anxiety grow within her gut. She sensed something dreadful was coming, and coming soon. She opened her eyes and attempted to shake off the eerie feeling that had overwhelmed her.

The grounds were well protected and reinforcements had been made to the estate as a result of the sporadic attacks. Though Adrian knew of the security upgrades, she was not any less apprehensive as certainly by now Lazigne and the twins had been made aware their prisoners had escaped. She continued to ponder the situation, "Surely they would be preoccupied with protecting themselves at the moment in preparation of Christians' revenge," she thought to herself. Adrian's eyes sprang open at the realization that Lucas and Christian were likely downstairs plotting at this very moment.

She sighed heavily as she stood from the tub and began to dress. She decided not to mention her insight just yet in hopes Christian and Lucas would take more time to recoup. Once eager, now she was concerned to see what the night would hold. Though Christian had been nothing but kind and patient with her, she knew that he was indeed a powerful and vicious Vampire. She feared he and Lucas would exact their revenge without having made proper preparation. "I need to get down there quickly," she thought as she rushed from the suite.

Adrian slowly opened the door where Lucas was being cared for and entered the room to find Christian sitting at his bedside. Relieved to see they were not preparing an attack she stood quietly as she watched the two of them calmly converse. Lucas appeared healthy and Christian was as gorgeous as ever, his appearance unblemished and the fierceness had more than returned to his eyes. She was elated to see him back in his normal state.

Christian turned toward the door as he had felt her presence. "Ah, there is my beautiful Adrian," he said as he stood. He walked to her and held her in his arms, releasing her only to kiss her softly on her lips.

"Not enough to make up for me waking to an empty bed," she smirked.

"We will have to work on that later," he said as he looked longingly into her eyes.

Christian took her by the hand and led them to Lucas' side.

"You look much better since I saw you last," she smiled. "How are you feeling, Lucas?" she asked as she placed her hand on his.

"I feel grateful to you for my life, how can I ever repay you?" he asked as he looked up into her eyes.

Adrian smiled, "Knowing you are recovering and are safe is payment enough," she said as she clung to Christian's arm.

Lucas weakly smiled at her response, "If anyone ever doubted your loyalty to Christian or to us, their minds are completely clear of that now," he said. Lucas turned to Christian as he continued, "There is but one gift I can give you," he said as he now returned his eyes to her. "You will feed from me once I am whole," he stated proudly.

Adrian tilted her head and bore an expression of confusion upon her face as a reaction to his statement. She wondered if he had begun to babble again. Lucas seeing the confusion on her face responded, "You were created by an elder; feeding on another elder will increase your abilities," he explained.

"This is a great honor," Christian added as he patted her hand lightly.

"Please excuse my ignorance on the matter, things have happened so quickly and there is so much I do not know or understand," she explained.

"My dear, there is no cause for you to apologize, you are cherished here for what you have done in the past as well as your most recent actions," he said as he held his hand out to her.

Adrian walked over to him and took his hand. "I am honored you feel that way," she said smiling. "I am very angry over what has happened in the past few weeks," she began. "I will have my revenge as will you, but for now it is important for you to rest," she said as she patted his hand while placing it back onto the bed.

Lucas smiled and nodded, "I am sure you and Christian have some lost time to make up for," he said as he settled deeply into the bed. With a nod of approval, Christian took her hand and led her from the room.

Christian closed the door gently behind them then backed her into the adjacent wall as he placed an unexpected and passionate kiss on her lips. Adrian sighed as he drew his face from hers, "Do not start what you can't finish," she said smiling.

"Who is it that says I cannot finish what I start?" Christian retorted as he smiled broadly.

He playfully swept her from her feet and within seconds they were entering his suite. He kicked the door closed behind them and carried her to the bed.

"I see you are better now," Adrian laughed, as she playfully wrapped her legs around his waist.

Christian smiled and kissed her passionately as he ran his fingers through her hair before slowly lifting his face from hers. "I thought of nothing but you while I was chained and locked away" he whispered. "The pain they inflicted upon me was nothing compared to the pain I felt at the thought of losing you for another eternity," he confessed.

She wrapped her arms around him pulling him closely to her, "I could not allow that to happen" she said as her eyes filled with tears. "I hate them for what they have done to us" she growled through her teeth, "I will torment them before I allow death to release them from their pain" she swore.

Christian wiped the tears from her eyes and kissed her forehead. He continued to place a line of kisses from her face to her neck and down her chest until her blouse obstructed him.

Christian had so missed making love to her; he grew excited in anticipation of feeling her soft skin against his body.

He slowly began to undress her as she lay submissively next to him. She observed him affectionately, his face alit with passion as he exposed her supple breasts; his eyes were fixed upon hers as he continued to remove her clothing.

Now lying naked before him, she reached up and began to remove his shirt as he lightly ran his fingertips over her eager breasts. She pulled him to her so that she could feel his bare chest against hers. "I missed this most I think," she whispered to him. "I love the way that your skin feels against mine," she finished.

Christian placed his hand behind her neck and flipped them over so that she was perched on top of him. She began to remove his pants as he lifted his head to take her left breast into his mouth. Adrian bit her lip as he gently sucked at her, she becoming eager to welcome him inside of her.

She coaxed him to lay his head down as she began to kiss his chest where the silver chains had burned themselves into him. Though there was no visible scar, she would forever remember the wounds that had been inflicted upon him. She continued to kiss him from his chest, down his stomach and across his groin. As she reached for his swollen manhood, he flipped them over once more, him now on top of her.

He gently stroked his hand down the length of her torso, stopping only to squeeze her left buttock before lifting her leg up and over his broad shoulder. Christian sighed heavily as he slowly inserted himself into her. Adrian arched her back and wrapped her arms around him. She gazed deeply into his dark eyes as he was staring down at her; ecstasy radiating from his face as his fangs began to protrude.

She rocked her hips slowly and gently with his. She felt her own fangs begin to protrude as Christian wrapped his arms tightly around her.

Their bodies began to rise from the bed as they passionately made love. Adrian, so consumed by their union, was oblivious to the fact that they no longer lay in the bed. She closed her eyes and began to breathe heavily just as Christian flipped them over. For one brief moment she was startled as the cold ceiling pressed firmly against her back.

His breath was now labored and she could feel that she was near orgasm as he began to plunge deeper and faster into her. Adrian spread her legs widely as he began to meet her with his own climax. He groaned as she rocked her hips frantically with his. Overwhelmed by passion, he sank his fangs into her shoulder. Adrian moaned as her body was enraptured in ecstasy; it was as if he had released some erotic venom into her when his fangs punctured her skin. Christian groaned loudly as her vagina pulsed around him. He clutched at her as his body shuddered with his release.

They slowly sank back down into the bed, Adrian now on top of him. Christian wrapped his arms about her, holding her closely he whispered, "I didn't mean to bite you."

Adrian smiled as she placed a kiss on his chest. "I liked it," she giggled.

Christian chuckled at her response, "So what shall we do with the remainder of our evening?" he asked as he brushed his hand across her pretty face.

Adrian rolled off of him and lay on her side with her leg draped over him. "We both should feed," she said, as she brushed her fingertips across his broad chest.

"I agree." Christian said as he reached to the nightstand to light a cigarette for them. "I have a place in mind, I think you will find the environment, well, interesting," he finished smiling slyly while handing her the cigarette.

Adrian tilted her head thoughtfully. "How, shall I dress?" she said grinning.

Christian took the cigarette back from her and rolled over on top of her, smiling broadly. "I prefer you undressed!" he teased.

She raised her head and kissed him passionately as she ran her hands down his back and onto his buttocks. "Such a great ass!" she said as she kissed him once more.

Christian enjoyed her playfulness but knew there were many things he needed to teach her. His expression shifted from bliss, his eyes reflected a deep concern and growing concern. She was a newly born vampire and in these perilous times she would need to know how to protect herself.

Christian slowly rolled onto his side next to her, "Have you mastered levitation?"

Adrian sat up erect in the bed and placed his head onto her thigh before answering, "I have levitated but it was involuntary. I was angry when it happened; it was during the vision of Daphne's attack." Adrian was lost momentarily as scenes from her vision came back to her. She shook the memories away and reached to retrieve the cigarette from Christian's hand, "Are you going to teach me?" she asked eagerly.

"I suppose so" he said as he rose from her lap, taking the cigarette from her to extinguish it in a nearby ashtray. Christian sat across from her in the bed. He struggled to stay on task as he admired her nude body. "Close your eyes and focus on the air around you," he began.

Adrian nodded and did as instructed.

"Know the air is heavier than you and you can move freely about it," he continued.

Adrian concentrated on his voice as she imagined she was hanging within the thick air that surrounded her body.

Christian smiled as Adrian's thin frame slowly began to rise from the bed. "It is within you to manipulate the direction and the speed with which you move," he said as she continued to float above him.

She stretched out her legs and began to hover above in a vertical position. Christian leaned back against the headboard smiling broadly; she learned quickly, which did not surprise him. Rarely had a newborn adapted at such a pace, yet Adrian had been no typical subject even in her mortal life. He continued to watch as Adrian focused intently on her task. She opened her eyes and smiled in delight as she now found she was in complete control. She began to dart about the room from one corner to the other, increasing her speed with each jump. Christian laughed; he visualized her as a child taking her first steps.

Abruptly, he sprang from the bed, cornering her against the ceiling. He laughed as he placed a kiss upon her forehead. "You learn quickly," he said. I am quite proud of you," he added. "You have been through so much pain and turmoil yet you seem only to grow stronger," he said as he brushed the hair from her eyes. "You shall become a very powerful vampire in your adolescence, I dread the day that you run into those that have caused us all of this heartache," he added as he continued to smile.

Christian began to lower them slowly to the floor. "You need to save your energy," he said, as he gently held her.

Adrian nodded and draped her arms around him as she placed a soft kiss upon his lips then pressed her body to his in a long embrace.

"Shower with me," he said as he pulled away just far enough to look into her eyes. Christian would easily become lost within her eyes when she was mortal but now that she was vampire they were even far more alluring. Within them he could see the innocence and wonder of a new Vampire but he could also see wisdom far beyond her years. There was more though; deep within her Christian could detect an undeniable sense of destiny, coupled with abilities that no Vampire had possessed for centuries.

Christian was abruptly rattled back into the present as Adrian leaned forward and kissed him. She took him by the hand and led them to the bathroom.

Adrian ran her hands down his chest as the water trickled down his muscular torso, inviting her hands to follow. He gently fondled her breasts as she place a deep kiss upon his lips. Slowly, he raised her leg over his hip as he pressed her back firmly against the wall of the shower.

She reached down and guided him into her as she lifted her other leg and crossed them tightly around him. He began to slowly thrust himself into her. She held herself up on his shoulders as she looked into his eyes. "I love you Christian," she said as she rocked her hips against his.

Christian was nearing climax, evident by the expression on his face. Adrian lifted her legs from him and wedged her feet against the opposite shower wall, allowing him a better and more stable position. Christian exploded within her immediately, "Adrian!" he panted as his orgasm neared its end.

Adrian lowered her legs beneath her and held him. "So much for that whole saving your energy thing-" she giggled.

Christian smiled as he placed a kiss on her lips. "Twenty four hours ago I was convinced I would never hold you again," he whispered breathlessly. "I will never let an opportunity pass me by to hold you or make love to you again," he added as he nuzzled his head into her shoulder, kissing her lightly.

Adrian returned his embrace as she whispered into his ear, "I will fight until death for you, and if you cannot be saved I will be happy to die with you." Christian was reminded of Cassandra's last words. He continued to hold tight to Adrian as he vowed to never leave her side again.

Chapter Eight

Soon after they were dressed and prepared for the evening. Christian escorted her out of the suite as he called for Markus to bring their car around.

"Let's go see Lucas before we leave," she said as they neared the bottom of the staircase. Christian nodded and reached down for her hand. They walked into the room where Lucas was being cared for to see him sitting upright in his bed and looking even stronger than he had earlier.

"Ah, good evening Ms. Adrian, Christian," he said smiling as he motioned for them to come closer.

"You look as though you are feeling much better," Adrian said as she reached out to embrace him.

"I am feeling much stronger indeed" Lucas responded enthusiastically. "And you, Christian, look to be as good as new" he smiled broadly.

Christian nodded in confirmation, "I was well taken care of" he smiled as he draped his arm around Adrian's waist.

"Where are you two off to this evening?" he asked.

"We are off to feed" Christian answered with no further details as he wished for their destination to be a surprise.

Lucas turned to Adrian "You seem to be adjusting well to our way of life, what say you?" Lucas asked curiously.

Adrian felt as though she were being tested, she chose her words carefully. "I am learning and Christian is helping me find my way" she replied graciously.

Lucas nodded his head; the expression on his face said he understood she still had some adjusting to do.

"Actually, she is progressing at an impressive rate," Christian bragged.

"Very good! Though I must admit that I am not surprised," Luca smiled. "You two go on about your way, come check in on me when you return," he finished.

Christian led her out of the room and to the main entrance where Markus stood waiting for them outside of the car.

"Good evening" he said as he opened the door for them.

"Good evening Markus" Adrian responded excitedly, "I've missed you, how are you this evening?"

"Just fine Miss, and I have missed you as well" he said smiling as she stooped to climb into the back seat. Christian slid in behind her just as Markus lowered his head into the door, "You had all of us very worried, I am overjoyed to see you well Miss."

"Thank you Markus, I am happy to be here," she smiled.

Markus nodded then backed away as he closed the car door.

"I think he's warming up to me," Adrian whispered.

Christian turned in his seat to face her, "He speaks the truth. During the time that you slept, he and the staff from both estates were beside themselves; there was never a moments peace!" he laughed. "Have no doubt Adrian, you are loved by many, including myself," he added as he draped his arm around her and pulled her near.

Adrian smiled warmly as she nuzzled against his broad chest, she knew she was right where she belonged despite any reservations that she may have had as a mortal.

The long black limo began to roll towards the main entrance. Christian leaned forward and poured wine for them, just as he had done on their first date. Adrian graciously accepted the glass and sipped at the pungent Merlot. "So tell me about where we are going" she prodded.

Christian sat back in his seat and draped his arm around her shoulder, "Don't be troubled," he said smiling as he read her thoughts. "The lifestyle of Vampire is a bit different here than it is in North America," he finished.

Adrian sighed, "I trust you, wherever we are going will be perfect as you will be by my side," she said smiling.

Christian pulled her closer to him and kissed her cheek. "I will never knowingly put you in harm's way," he said as his fingers twirled about in her hair.

Adrian crossed her legs over his lap as she sipped her wine, she was so content to be in his arms again she had not focused further on their enemy or their heinous acts; there would be a time for that in the very near future.

Adrian watched through the front windshield as the car rolled down the scenic narrow roads. The night sky was clear with a nearly full moon lighting the terrain that surrounded them. Now having driven through the city of Grenoble, the scenery became dark and desolate. Soon the car turned down a small paved road that wound through a heavily wooded field. Shortly after, they rolled to a stop in front of an old, crumbling stone farmhouse.

Markus drove to the rear of the house where a digital keypad stood before a garage door. He entered a code and the door began to rise, exposing a brightly-lit concrete parking garage that was near to capacity.

"What the hell!" Adrian exclaimed.

Christian chuckled at her response as he placed their empty wine glasses back into the rack in preparation of leaving the car. Markus parked in a spot near to an elevator marked "V.I.P." and exited the car to open the door for them.

Christian held his hand out to her once he stood. "I assure you that you are in for a surprise this evening," he smiled. As she joined him, he took her arm and escorted her to the ornate elevator, which Markus had already summoned for them.

The doors slid open to reveal a work of art. Adrian stood quietly as she admired the golden trim and etchings that adorned its' inner walls. She was so mesmerized by the intricacy of the etchings that she had hardly noticed the length of the ride down and was startled as the elevator settled and the doors slid open.

Adrian gawked in disbelief, before her was an enormous and elaborately decorated nightclub. There were crystal chandeliers and golden trim as far as the eye could see. There were several bars, neon lights, dance floors and private sitting areas all décorated in Victorian style furnishings. She peered to see inside one of the sitting areas; though the sheer curtains were drawn, she could make out a male Vampire feeding upon two nude females. The women, which Adrian instinctively identified as mortals, seemed to enjoy his feeding upon them. She found the scene quite erotic as she continued to observe. The humans writhed in ecstasy as the vampire would suckle from one to the other.

Though she had begun to feel aroused she turned her questioning gaze to Christian, who immediately responded to her. "There is a different mentality amongst our kind here," he said as he smiled down at her.

She was contented by his comment and drew her arm up and around his as he escorted her through the booming establishment. She noted as they walked through the crowd that there was a mixture of Vampire and human alike. Everyone looked upon Christian as if they knew him, bowing their heads as he passed by. The crowd widened a path for them as they approached, and Adrian heard their thoughts - thoughts of her, concerns over the ongoing attacks and rumors of wars amongst the clans. Though she could hear their thoughts, she had not once felt as though they had attempted to read hers. She grew concerned that perhaps they were and she was not experienced enough to notice. Christian leaned to her and whispered, "They would not dare" in response to her ponderings.

"Why?" she asked as she looked up at him. Christian smiled at her innocence as he responded, "Firstly, because you are my mate, secondly because you have my blood, the blood of an elder within you," he finished as he kissed her forehead.

With his response she began to realize his position within the Vampire population, as well as her own. She returned to taking in her surroundings but was soon distracted by a man in the distance as he called Christian out by name.

A short male Vampire in a tuxedo was rushing towards them. "Lord Christian, we are so pleased to have you here!" he said breathlessly as he approached. "And this must be Adrian" he exclaimed. "You are as beautiful the rumors say," he added as he reached for her hand and bowed to her.

Adrian was taken aback. She looked deeply into his eyes as he neared, she sensed that he was sincere in his actions. "Thank you," she said, as she slowly drew her hand back from his.

"May I escort you to your seating area Lord?" he asked eagerly.

Christian nodded in confirmation as they followed the tuxedo-clad Vampire to a private seating area that faced a conformingly elaborate stage.

Adrian took her seat on a large overstuffed velvet couch with golden feet and arms. She had hardly settled before a waitress appeared from nowhere. The girl bowed reverently before pouring a glass of champagne for she and Christian then turned to place the bottle in a chiller before leaving. Christian sat next to her, as he thanked their escort.

"If there is anything that you would require Lord, please don't hesitate to ask," the man said, as he bowed and left them in peace.

Christian wrapped his arm around her and kissed her softly as he handed her a glass of champagne. They toasted together and sipped their drinks just as exotic dancers filed onto the stage to perform for them.

Adrian watched on as the young girls danced, surprised by the fact she was not uncomfortable with their presence; in fact she found that she was rather aroused.

Christian pulled her close to him and whispered in her ear, "Select your donor."

Adrian was not stunned by his comment; she had already begun to understand and accept the goings-on that surrounded her.

"I want to watch them for a little while first," she said as she focused on the dancers.

She leaned back into the plush couch and sipped at her champagne as she shifted even closer to him. After a few moments she pointed at a young auburn-haired girl. She found she was attracted to the curves of her slender body; her skin was perfect, like ivory. Adrian imagined she would taste sweet to her. The realization crossed her mind once more; she was no longer human. She now was forced to acknowledge the changes within her; such a thought would have never entered her mortal mind.

She sipped heavily at her champagne as Christian motioned for the girl to come to them. The young girl smiled and began to approach stopping only to close the sheer curtains as she entered the seating area.

Slowly she turned to approach them, smiling as she knelt at Adrian's feet.

Adrian looked to Christian as the girl bowed, placing her arms in Adrian's lap with her wrists facing up.

Christian nodded as he motioned to the girl, "Feed," he said encouragingly.

She leaned over to place her glass on the table then lifted the young girl's left wrist to her mouth; her skin smelled sweet, a hint of the flavor within her, just as she had imagined. Adrian could hear the girl's blood pulsing madly throughout her body yet her heart held a slow and steady rhythm.

She stroked the girl's arm as she gently punctured her ivory skin and began to drink. The blood was warm and thick as it coated her throat, sating the hunger within her. Immediately she could feel the donor's blood pulse through her veins. Adrian sensed the girl was aroused, which in turn aroused her. She was surprised at herself, as she had never been attracted a woman as a mortal.

The girl remained in her bowed position until Adrian had had her fill. She placed her arm back down into her lap; the girl then stood slowly, smiling seductively at Adrian as before departing the seating area.

Adrian wiped her mouth as she watched the girl's naked frame disappear into the crowd. She turned her attention to Christian, who was smiling proudly at her having publicly fed.

Adrian lifted her glass of champagne to him and drank to rinse the remaining blood from her mouth. Without another word being said, Christian raised his hand and pointed to another dancer, motioning her over to them.

She entered the room and knelt at Christian's feet just as the first girl had. Christian looked into Adrian's eyes as he drank from her. Adrian found it very arousing to watch. He lifted the girl's other arm and offered it to her, never breaking their eye contact.

Adrian accepted and fed briefly from her as she gazed deeply into his eyes. Christian soon released the girl's arm, as he had drunk his fill. The girl rose from her knees and bowed her head slightly to them before turning to leave.

Adrian, having become more comfortable with the environment, selected a third donor and motioned her over to them. Together they fed on seven separate donors throughout the night.

Their hunger sated, Christian and Adrian decided to leave the establishment for the evening. While in the elevator, Adrian turned to Christian, "Are there no places like this in the States?" she asked.

"There are but two," he replied. "I own both of them, one in New Orleans the other in New York." Just then the elevator doors opened to reveal Markus awaiting them.

He hurried to the back of the car and ushered them in, closing the door behind them. Once in the car, Markus asked, "Where will we be going next?"

Christian looked to Adrian for an answer. "I prefer to go back to the estate so we can check on Lucas" she answered.

"Miss Adrian prefers to go home Markus," Christian tolled. Markus nodded in response and the car began to roll forward.

"So, did you find your experience this evening enjoyable?" Christian asked.

She thought briefly before responding. "I enjoyed it and found several elements quite erotic; for example, watching you feed on the female."

"Did you now?" he asked smiling broadly as he pulled her closer to him.

Adrian turned to him and placed her hand on his chest, "I think I was jealous it was she who was holding your attention, and not me," she said teasingly.

Christian placed his hand under her chin and drew her face to his as he kissed her softly. She ran her hands through his hair and pulled his head back, exposing his neck to her. Gently she began to brush her lips against his neck when suddenly she grew wretched with fear.

Adrian sprung up erect in the seat, Christian now feeling the same surge. They both knew that the estate was under attack.

"Stop the car!" she ordered. Markus slammed on the brakes and turned back in his seat to see what the matter was. Adrian held her head as the scene began to materialize. "They're at the main entrance," she screeched as she looked up at Christian.

"Are you up to this?" Christian asked.

He was conflicted on whether he should rush to the estate, knowing that she would demand to follow, or flee out of concern for her safety.

Adrian answered without hesitation, "Lucas must still be protected, let's go!" Markus slammed the accelerator to the floor and raced toward the estate.

Christian nodded and reached forward for the headrest of the seat next to them. He lifted a panel revealing three levers then flipped the middle lever.

Adrian watched as the leather panel behind the bar was beginning to slide open, revealing a small arsenal. There were swords and an assortment of large handguns. "Ladies first," he smiled as he waved his hand towards the stash.

Adrian smiled as she chose a 9mm and a sword.

Christian selected a dagger, two handguns and a sword as well.

Markus attempted to reach someone at the estate to warn them of the impeding threat as he drove. Having been only a couple of miles from the estate, Markus sped to a wooded area just outside of the main entrance. The three of them exited the car and stood in the thicket as they organized their attack. Deciding to pick off as many as they could quietly from behind and work their way forward they set off for the main gate.

Chapter Nine

Adrenalin surged through her body as she watched the guards fight to hold off the intruders at the gate. She momentarily tore her eyes from the guards to see that there was activity near the estate as well. In a panic she turned behind herself to see Markus trailing off into the trees with a sniper rifle slung over his shoulder, Christian was now speeding towards her.

"Stay behind me!" Christian said as he drew his sword and charged toward the gate. Adrian smirked at his comment before following his lead.

Christian and Adrian began to dart back and forth behind the enemy lines. Adrian drew her sword and chose her first victims. Viciously she swung her blade as she appeared behind them one by one, leaving a trail of headless bodies in her path. The invaders were now caught between Christian and Adrian and the guards, who fought indiscriminately through their ranks. The intruders fired blindly, as they did not know from which direction they would be attacked.

Bullets were flying about them, Adrian looked to her left just as one of their guards was struck. Remembering their sense of loyalty to both herself and Christian she became infuriated.

Adrian stopped in her tracks as she watched the guard slump to the ground. Her blood began to boil; she would certainly vindicate this loss. She turned in the direction from where the shot had been fired to see an armed intruder in the tree line. Just as she spotted him, he fired on her and struck her in her left arm. She felt the bullet burn through her. Taking note of the wound, she allowed her fury to overtake her.

She found her pain only fueled her anger. She leered at the sniper and sped towards him, suddenly appearing directly in front of him. Snatching his rifle from his hands, she glared into his eyes and bared her fangs at him as she reached up and snapped his neck. The sniper crumpled to the ground at her feet. Adrian sneered down at the corpse then kicked it aside as if it were rubbish. She looked to her wound again to see that it had begun to close.

Still angered from being shot, she rushed back to the gate to find Christian organizing the guards as the entrance had been secured. Just as she appeared at Christian's side, half of the guards split off and headed to the estate while the other half formed a new line of defense at the gate. Christian reached down and placed his hand on her wound. "Are you alright?" he asked.

"I'm pissed!" she said as she turned her gaze to the estate. "Shall we?" she asked as she turned her fierce eyes back to him.

"Indeed" Christian growled.

They headed across the lawn, through the smoke-ridden night air towards the estate. They arrived to find the steel shutter on the front door pulled from its tracks. Christian looked at Adrian, "They've gotten inside," he growled.

Adrian turned to the guards, "Position yourselves here. If anyone comes out, kill them!" she said, as they squeezed through the opening.

Everything was as it was when they had left earlier that evening, but it was eerily quiet inside of the estate. Adrian assumed all had made it to the lower levels and were safe. They began to walk through the long corridor to inspect the bottom floor. Suddenly, the sound of footsteps descending the stairs emerged from the silence.

She and Christian crouched down on either side of the corridor, just out of sight of the intruder. Adrian peered around the corner to see whose footsteps they had heard. "Aramond," she whispered across to Christian.

Christian's face distorted into a scowl. Aramond froze in his tracks, as he had sensed their presence. Adrian motioned for Christian to cross over to her. As he approached, she motioned to him that she would go around and wait for Aramond to reach the bottom of the stairs. Christian nodded as she sped to crouch in the second corridor to await Aramond's descent.

Aramond grinned slyly as he sped from the stairs towards the front entrance where, he would be met by the guards. As he stopped at the door to squeeze his way out, Christian sprang from the corridor with his sword drawn.

Aramond, sensing his approach and turned just as Christian appeared behind him. Christian swung his sword as Aramond's eyes met his. Aramond's head fell to the floor with a solid thud.

Adrian rose from her hiding spot and walked over to see the headless body. "One down" she grinned, as Christian wiped his sword across Aramond's broad chest.

"I think we should split up" she said as she looked away from the severed head. "I will take the second level and meet you back down here once I have checked it out" she said.

Christian begrudgingly agreed, only because he knew he would sense it if she were to find any trouble.

Adrian disappeared up the stairwell before he could say another word. Stealthily she made her way through the corridors. All the doors appeared to still be shuttered, with the exception of Christian's suite. She slowly slid in through the opening and surveyed the room. Nothing appeared to have been disturbed and no one was there. She walked back out of the suite cautiously and made her way down the remainder of the corridor, checking all other doors as she went.

Having found no other disturbances, she made her way back down the stairwell and into the foyer. With no sign of Christian, she continued through the main level, securing each room as she proceeded. She made her way across the foyer and towards the Parliament doors. Sensing motion inside, she slowly opened the door and saw that Devionne, Aramond's twin brother, was pinned to the floor by Christian's sword. Christian knelt beside him was questioning him on his agenda. Adrian, noticing that an old leather bound book lay on the floor at Devionne's feet. She walked over to retrieve it as Christian hovered over him with his hand clutching at Devionne's throat.

Adrian glanced down at Devionne. "He will not answer you," she said as she looked into his eyes. She leaned over him and snatched a gold chain from his neck. Christian looked down at Devionne and sneered, "Now you're fucked!"

Adrian, looked at him and shouted quickly, "Don't kill him!" Christian looked at her questioningly. "I want to feed from him," she stated calmly as she sat nearby and began to focus on the gold chain.

Christian smiled broadly at her request as he pushed down further on the sword to insure Devionne would not escape. "I am not certain that his blood is befitting of such as honor, however, it will be as you have requested," Christian taunted as he looked down at Devionne.

"He came here for you and Lucas, and this book," Adrian began. "They were sent by Lazigne - twenty-four in all. We should have the guards count the bodies to make sure that we got all of them," she announced.

"There are two panel trucks parked near the hangar," she continued. "Lazigne is in Italy now," she said. Devionne spun his head and glared at her as she continued. "They are gathering within the next seventy-two hours to form a mass attack on this estate." They had intended on breaching us without having been detected tonight," she added.

Adrian broke her trance and looked to Christian. "Though the men that came here are all dead, we do still have the element of surprise on our side if the attack is pursued," she said as she stood. Adrian walked over to Devionne and knelt gingerly at his side.

"Your accomplices will meet a horrific demise. Thank you for the information," she grinned.

Devionne now wore an expression of both fear and frustration upon his face as she leaned over him. He struggled to free himself, hissing and spitting towards her. Adrian, now hovering over his face, grinned broadly. "Fuck you!" she said before violently sinking her fangs into his broad chest. Adrian ripped at his flesh with her fingernails as she fed from him. She left him still alive as she stood and walked away.

Christian placed his foot on Devionne's chest as he withdrew his sword. With one swift blow, Christian removed his head. He leaned over briefly and wiped the blood from his weapon before turning to follow Adrian.

"We must evacuate the Parliament," he said as they made their way down the corridor and to the hidden access that led to the lower levels.

"I agree, but at this point, where would they be housed could be considered safe?" she pondered aloud. Christian tightened his lips at her query as he realized he had no response.

They descended the dank stairs and began to call for Naomi and Ruth, thinking it might be in their best interests to alert them of their presence. Naomi answered shortly after.

"We are here," she called from a small room at the bottom of the stairs.

"Is everyone present and accounted for?" Christian asked. "Yes, Markus called us just as the guards at the entrance alerted us of the attack," she responded.

Adrian could see Lucas seated in a large chair at the back of the room. He motioned for her to come to him.

"How is it we continue to be in your debt?" he asked smiling.

"You are looking well, Lucas," she responded, "and you are in no one's debt," she added. She leaned forward and placed a kiss on his cheek. "I am happy to see that you have recovered," she said as Christian joined then.

"We have to evacuate the estate," he announced.

Christian explained everything that had happened since their return earlier that evening, the elders listening attentively.

As Christian ended his report, Lucas stood up from his chair. "I will not run from them," he announced.

Christian hung his head, as he knew there would be no point in arguing.

"If this is the stance that you choose, we must prepare the estate for heavy attacks," Adrian responded. "We should send for the remaining elders, as well as their security staff," she began as she stared blankly away. "We need to repair the damaged shutters, obtain silver munitions for the assault rifles, and most importantly, devise a plan," she added. "The other elders will take the same stance as Lucas; wouldn't it be wise that we stand together?" she finished.

Christian stood with his mouth agape at her response.

Lucas, noting his expression, began to chuckle. "Something tells me that this estate will not suffer the same fate as the others," he said, smiling. "We shall meet back up in the chambers and begin our planning," he continued.

Christian stopped him in mid-sentence, "First, we need to get the body count from Security, I will make sure that all 24 are present and accounted for before you leave the caverns," he announced. Lucas lowered himself back into his chair to await the results from Christian, who had already left the room.

Adrian's mind was in overdrive planning for the attack. Soon after, Christian had made his way back and announced all bodies were recovered and had been loaded into the trucks that had been parked near the hangar.

"The bodies should be dumped somewhere where they can be easily discovered and we need to fortify the gate and front entrance immediately to erase any signs of them having been here tonight" Adrian stated bluntly.

Christian and Lucas both were surprised by how Adrian was responding to the situation at hand, her thoughts were calculating and precise. Feeding from both Christian and Devionne had heightened her knowledge of battle plans and defense.

"If it appears as though their men were attacked elsewhere, it could buy us some time as Lazigne will be distracted as he searches in vain for those responsible," she mumbled as she paced.

Knowing she was right, Christian ordered security to drive the trucks into the city and park them outside of a well-known nightclub.

As the staff made their way out of the lower levels, Christian, Adrian and the elders followed them and met up in the Parliament chambers.

Ruth began to make contact with the remaining elders to alert them of the situation and have them relocate immediately to the Grenoble Estate to prepare for the attack.

Naomi took charge of all required repairs and cleanup to the estate, as they would need to appear unscathed.

Adrian began making a list of munitions that they would require while Christian and Lucas determined where security would be positioned and explored optional tactics in their defense.

By mid-morning, all plans had been made, the estate appeared as it did prior to the attack. All elders were en route with their security staffs and William had been sent to obtain the items from Adrian's munitions list. The first of the elders were expected to arrive within the hour, and the remaining ten would follow sporadically throughout the day. Adrian recommended placing a heavy guard around the hangars, as they would not be able to leave their jets until dusk.

Exhausted and with nothing more to do but wait, Christian and Adrian decided to retire to their suite for some much-needed rest, as there would be much to do in the coming hours.

Adrian awoke with her arm draped over Christian's chest. She laid contently next to him, watching him sleep peacefully for a while before deciding to get out of bed. Slowly she crept across the room and selected some clean clothes from her suitcase so that she could shower before he awoke. As the warm water trickled over her naked body, her thoughts were scattered between the impending attacks; she wondered if the bodies of the intruders had been discovered. Her mind then shifted as she mentally reviewed the munitions list to determine if she had overlooked anything. She was becoming overwhelmed by the situation that they were in once again.

There is too much to be done for me to be in the shower, she sighed, as she turned off the water and began to dry her body.

She dressed herself and turned to leave the room. As her eyes landed on Christian, who was still sleeping soundly, she remembered how she felt when she awoke to an empty bed. She determined that she would not do the same to him, especially in these troubled times. She smiled adoringly as she stared at him, and decided to crawl back into the bed to lay near him for just a few minutes more. As she settled next to him he began to stir.

"Hello Beautiful," he said, as he focused his eyes on her.

Adrian smiled as she stroked his cheek. "Hi," she whispered as she placed a kiss on his forehead.

"Have you been awake long?" he asked.

"No, not really., I was going to go downstairs, but then I looked at you still sleeping and I didn't want you to wake alone, so I had just laid back down next to you."

Christian sat up in the bed and admired her. "That was very thoughtful of you," he smiled as he stared into her beautifully fierce eyes. "I would have been worried if I had woken up and you were gone," he finished as he placed his hand on her thigh. Christian rolled over on top of her and kissed her passionately. He raised himself upon his elbows so that he could look down upon her. "I adore you Adrian," he smiled. "I want you to know how proud you have made me in the past few days," he said, as he continued to gaze into her eyes.

"I've only done what I thought you would do in the same situation," she said smiling back at him.

Christian lowered his head and kissed her lightly on the neck.

"You are starting something we don't have time to finish Christian," she sighed. "We have far too much to do" she reminded him.

He slowly lifted up and placed his forehead against hers. "You're right," he admitted with a tone of disappointment in his voice.

"You should take that sexy ass of yours and get dressed so that you can meet me downstairs," she said laughingly.

Christian smirked at her as he stood from the bed and made his way to the shower, removing his clothes as he crossed the room.

Adrian licked her lips as she ogled his nude body. "Oh, fuck it!" she said, as she jumped from the bed and chased after him.

Christian laughed as he lifted her from the ground and made his way back to the bed with her in his arms. Adrian began to remove her clothes and threw them across the room on top of his. She pressed her naked body against his as her hands caressed his broad shoulders. Christian flung her into the bed and landed on top of her playfully as she wrapped her legs tightly around his waist. She brushed his lips with hers, teasing him with each light touch.

Christian began to pry his way into her, she adjusting her hips to welcome him. He rolled them over, leaving her atop him. She aggressively pinned his arms while she slowly raised and lowered herself onto him, each stroke slower and longer.

Suddenly he sat upright with her in his lap, placed his hands on her hips, and began to manipulate her speed. Adrian threw her head back as her body began to tingle, alerting her to an upcoming orgasm. Christian began to increase the pace as she thrust herself down onto him. With each stroke, she began to cry out to him as her body writhed in ecstasy. He reached up and wrapped his hand around her throat, increasing the intensity of her orgasm. As her vagina pulsed around his swollen cock, she reached for his hand and drew it to her mouth, sucking his fingers as her orgasm abated.

Christian rolled them over once more and mounted her. She drew her legs up against his chest and crossed her ankles around his neck, prompting him to climax. His body convulsed as she tightened her legs around him, his eyes closed in passion as his orgasm now began to subside.

Christian collapsed on top of her, breathless and spent. Adrian loved to know that she satisfied him as well as he did her. She caressed his head as he lay on her chest. She enjoyed holding him in this fragile state. He so fierce and knowing, yet now lay defenseless in her arms.

"I suppose that you should shower with me-" he chuckled.

"I suppose so-" she said, laughing as she slapped his naked ass.

With no more time to lose, they were both dressed and on their way down to the chambers within minutes.

Christian opened the massive and elaborately-carved wooden doors to find that most of the elders were present and in deep conversation. Adrian followed as he entered the room.

Frederick was the first to notice them, "Ah, Christian and the lovely Ms. Adrian - so good to see you both again." He smiled as he stood up and walked towards them with his arms spread to welcome them.

The other elders quieted their conversations, as they had noted Christian and Adrian's presence. Lucas looked up from the table where he sat and motioned for them to join him. "Let's get you two up to speed" he said.

Christian nodded as he pulled a seat away from the table for Adrian, quickly seating himself beside her in order to begin.

All members of the Parliament now gathered, the room grew silent in anticipation of planning for the impending attack.

Lucas shared the opinions of the other elders with Christian and Adrian and then opened the table for discussion. Within a short period it seemed that the Parliament had devised a plan to defend the estate and had vowed to capture and kill all of the opposing clans.

Isaac had been silent through most of the discussions but his civil nature required for him to speak. "We are a civilized nation. Should the captured not have a trial?" he asked.

Most of the elders smirked at his words. Adrian found she could not control her tongue.

"Excuse my brazenness, but if they are captured here, on these grounds, and they are armed, they obviously didn't come for tea," she said. Adrian clamped her mouth shut as she cast her eyes down to the table before her. She was surprised at herself for having blurted out her thoughts.

She glanced apologetically toward Christian who was struggling not to laugh at her outburst. The room grew silent.

"My apologies" she said, as she visually acknowledged each elder.

After another moment of silence Isaac spoke again "I suppose you are right" he said as he humbly returned to his seat.

Christian chuckled under his breath; Adrian lifted her head to see Frederick and Christian's eyes locked as they had both laughed at her outburst. She glanced across the room, and was relieved to see that Lucas wore the same expression on his face.

Christian took it upon himself to introduce a new topic. "How are the improvements to the exterior coming?" he asked.

Naomi stood and gave her report. "All openings have had a second layer of steel shutters added, the roof has had iron barricades installed, cameras have been installed throughout the grounds, and there are 365 trained guards on the property as we speak."

"What about the munitions?" Adrian asked.

"Ah, munitions are my forte," Frederick said as he stood. "William contacted me late last night," he began. "We are expecting a delivery here at any moment" he said as he placed his hands upon the table and leaned towards the group smiling.

"Sounds like we are prepared" Christian said, as he looked at Adrian who was deep in thought. Realizing Christian was looking at her as he spoke, she lifted her head and asked, "What was the relevance of the book that Devionne had when Christian found him?" An eerie silence overtook the room as the question left her lips. The elders looked to each other silently as they were hesitant to elaborate.

Lucas stood from the table, approached Christian and placed a hand on his shoulder as he leaned to whisper, "Perhaps you should explain the book to her." Lucas smiled nervously at Adrian as he stood and returned to his seat.

Christian sighed as he offered her his arm. She looked up to him, confused over the reaction of the elders to her seemingly innocent question. She took Christians arm, following him as he led her into Lucas' study.

"What the hell!" Adrian said as she looked at him questioningly. Christian closed the door and motioned for her to sit on the couch.

He rubbed his brow and paced the floor as he began "The book has existed for centuries because we have protected it; it is considered taboo to even speak of it" he began. It is a compilation of spells can be used in conjunction with Vampire blood." Though he had hoped the broad description would sate her, Christian saw that Adrian wanted nothing less than a full explanation.

He sighed as he continued. "The roots of this book date back to the temples in ancient Egypt," he said as he sat next to her. "The Priests were liaison to the Vampire race. Those known as Gods of that time were our kind, they shared their knowledge, and their blood with these Priests who in turn integrated the worship of blood into Egyptian society."

"There is unfathomable knowledge within those pages, secrets that mankind should never know," he said as he stood. "The book also contains rites and incantations that would be very dangerous if they were to fall into the wrong hands. Legends have told of the insurmountable evil born of these rites, so the book has been hidden safely amongst us, until now," he sighed.

Adrian sat quietly waiting for more to be said.

"The fact of the matter is the spells do work and in the hands of our enemies it could be devastating to our civilization," he ended. Christian stood quietly and awaited her response.

"Have you read this book?" Adrian asked. "Bits and pieces of it," he responded shortly.

Adrian sat quietly for a moment more. "What is it that you are not telling me?" she prodded.

Christian returned to his seat beside her and began to explain, "Yesterday, when Lucas told you that he would allow you to feed on him, remember that I told you it was a great honor?"

"Yes" she answered.

Christian continued, "There is a rite in this book that requires a new Vampire to feed on the blood of three elders. The recipient acquires strength and abilities with unknown bounds. Such a powerful Vampire would be the greatest ally or the undefeatable enemy. For this reason the book has been the well-guarded secret of our kind since it was penned. This action would make one of us truly eternally undead and virtually indestructible," he finished.

"I see," she said as she sat imagining the threat that would exist had the rogue clan gotten their hands on it. "That explains why they did not kill you and Lucas," she mumbled. She pondered for a moment more before forming her opinion, "No one Vampire should have that kind of power," she concluded.

Christian stood and breathed a sigh of relief, "Then we are of the same understanding," he said as he held his hand out to her.

"Is there anything in that book that would help us through our situation?" she asked.

Christian stood motionless for a moment and then responded, "No one Vampire has been allowed to read the entire book. I have read part, and Isaac and Lucas have read the remainder of the book and in the past we have collaborated our findings. We consider the book dangerous, as there is too much truth within its pages," he said as he shifted in his chair.

Adrian stood for a moment, and perceived that his answer was not an answer. "I understand your position; however, between you, Isaac and Lucas, you have knowledge of these spells, and if there is something there that will help us, I believe it would be unacceptable not to use the knowledge you have," she said in conclusion.

Christian turned to face her. "There is truth in what you say, but the Parliament is very traditional and will have great difficulty in allowing us to use the rites in the book. We have guarded it for so long that it has become legend to most. The elders will be hesitant to breathe new life into its existence. Perhaps we should express this to Lucas in private," he suggested as he leaned to kiss her forehead.

"It seems to me that the book was more than legend to those who came to retrieve it," she stated adamantly as she turned in his direction.

Christian hung his head and sighed, "I suppose that is a quite valid point," he surrendered.

Christian stood to lead them from the study and back into the chambers, where the elders had now separated into small groups as they planned for the next day. Adrian spotted Lucas and Isaac in deep conversation in the back of the room. She slowly approached them as not to intrude.

Lucas sensing she wanted to speak with him, diverted his attention to her as an end to his present conversation.

"Ah, Ms. Adrian, you're troubled, what can I do?" he asked smiling warmly at her.

Adrian carefully chose her words before proceeding; "Please excuse me if I am out of line, as I have much to learn," she began. "Christian has explained the importance of the book to me and I understand why it is so guarded. However, in my eyes it would be wrong not to use the knowledge within in it to protect our clan as you have protected it, this in knowing that the twins had been sent to retrieve it; it is no longer hidden from the world."

Isaac and Lucas stood frozen at her suggestion. Adrian continued to stand adamantly before them awaiting their response. Lucas sat quietly as he began to consider her observation.

"Perhaps you are right," he admitted, "but I will have great difficulty convincing the other elders of this, no matter how valid your point," he said as he pecked his fingernails onto the table in front of him. "I will call a meeting in order to discuss this immediately," he proclaimed.

Lucas stood and called for the elders to follow him into his study. Christian smiled, shaking his head as he glanced at Adrian before leaving with them.

Adrian found herself alone in the room with all of the heads of Security. They gathered in one corner discussing their plans for stationing the guards around the estate and what munitions would be used where. Out of boredom, she decided to go back to the suite and have a cigarette and glass of wine; surely this meeting would not end any time soon.

Adrian settled into the large Victorian chair near the bed as she lit a cigarette and sipped at her wine. She began to consider all means of access to the estate and any tactics that would be used by the rogue clans. Most important to her now was the safety of the book, even over the safety of the elders. She thought carefully of a good hiding place for it and determined that she might suggest tucking it away somewhere within the caverns beneath the estate. She began to wrack her brain as she mentally organized all that needed to be done for their protection when, suddenly, the thought of her being back at her office and surrounded by her staff called all her thoughts to a sudden halt.

She missed her job and her friends; she wondered how they might react if they knew what and where she was now - all except for Jenny. Jenny had been accepting of her, no matter what. Her heart ached at the loss of her friend, which in turn filled her once more with rage. She was more than ready to inflict her vengeance on those that had caused her to lose her friends, her life and her beloved pet. She found herself clawing at the arm of the chair in anger; the beautifully carved wooden arm snapped into splinters before she could stop herself.

"Shit, now look what I've done!" she laughed, as she admired her own strength. She stood from her seat and looked down at the splintered armrest then was suddenly struck with the feeling that the meeting below had adjourned.

Chapter Ten

Upon reaching the bottom of the stairs, she looked up to see the Elders leaving Lucas' study. Their hushed whispers suggesting that the conversation had been a heated one.

Christian and Lucas were the last to exit. Still involved in deep conversation, Christian had not noticed her standing and waiting for him. Adrian followed the crowd back into the chambers to see what decision had been made. She slid in through the doors behind Lucas and stood anxiously in the rear of the chambers as she listened to the elders, who had now begun squabbling amongst themselves.

The air was thick with anxiety as Lucas called the room to order; all of them sat silently behind their solemn faces. Adrian approached Christian, who was still deeply involved in conversation with Lucas. He turned to her as she placed her arm around his.

"It seems that, once again, I have caused quite a stir," she said nervously. Christian chuckled at her observation, "Who would expect anything less of you?" he asked.

Lucas chuckled at the two of them before addressing her query. "Begrudgingly, the elders have decided you have a point," he nodded. "We have protected the book for centuries; now is the time for the book to protect us."

Lucas, now seated behind the towering podium began to address the members of Parliament, "The task at hand is to study the formulas and rites therein in search of something that will assist us in protecting the estate" he began. "Let it be known that on this night the Parliament has ordered the book unsealed!" He added. Each member will receive a portion the book out in order to do this in a timely manner; this is to include Miss Adrian," he said as he glanced in her direction.

Adrian could sense this had not been a unanimous decision from the group; in fact, several members were angered she had been given the honor of reading from the book. Adrian shook off the distraction and focused on Lucas in order to respond appropriately.

"I am honored," she said, as she absorbed his words and their implications.

"William and Ruth are dividing the book as we speak," Christian said, as he motioned across the room.

All of the elders were soon standing around a large table intently watching as the aged and brittle pages were being handed out. Each elder would reverently accept their portion and be seated somewhere within the chambers to begin their studies.

"Shall we?" Lucas smiled as he motioned for them to relocate to the sprawling table.

The three of them sat and awaited their portion. William laid Adrian's portion on the table before her. She could feel a strange vibration coming from its withering pages, something similar to the feeling that she had upon she and Christian's first encounter.

Adrian touched the pages and immediately began to see flashes of the Priests within their darkened abodes beneath the ancient temples. She was drawn to the figure a tall thin man in a long, hooded black robe standing near an altar. An eerie blue flame burned atop it, emitting just enough light to reveal the scene. She watched on as the Priest held his arms outward; she could hear mumbling but could not make out what was being said. As quickly as the vision appeared, it was gone. She was left with the feeling that the man was very powerful and feared, not a feeling of evil but of something else that she could not determine.

Adrian shook off the remnants of the vision and began to examine the pages of the book, written in some ancient language on one side with translations in Old English on the opposite. She would hold her hand on the ancient text as she read the translation to ensure that she understood the writings correctly.

Everyone at the table was deeply engrossed in their readings. The room was silent, with the exception of the shuffling sounds of the aged pages as they were being turned. Adrian found her section quite droning so far, as it referenced astronomical charts and constellations. She continued to read further, hoping for a change in topic.

Ruth suddenly disturbed the silence, as she felt that she had discovered something helpful. "There is a potion here that requires the blood of the maker in order to draw strength from all of those that were turned by him," she mumbled coherently. "I can't see that working for us," she sighed as she flipped to the next page. All heads that had lifted to hear her now returned their focus on the pages before them.

Adrian continued her reading as well. As she flipped to the next page, there was a drawing of a beast with skin of armor breathing fire and wielding a giant sword; the translation below it read: "The eternal one."

The book had now gained her attention, as this must have been what Christian had warned her about earlier. Adrian ran her hand over the drawing and began to feel the beast was quite evil, a chill straightened her spine before she could remove her hand from the book. She shook off the dreadful sensation as she continued her task. The writings went on to say that a new Vampire turned by an elder would require feeding from two additional elders under the light of a full moon. She noticed what appeared to be an incantation in the ancient text had not been translated into Old English. After having been informed of how feared the book had been, she understood why the translation was not available. She continued to read further. The remaining translation warned that a subject would gain strength and knowledge possessed by none before, along with other untold abilities. The rite was based upon the legend of one called Apocolieus.

A story followed, Apocolieus as a new Vampire, was turned during a time of war by his lover Heliah who had been a ranking member of the elders of her time, and had saved Apocolieus from mortal death, as he had been wounded while he was protecting her and her clan. The stronghold of the clan was infiltrated that evening and Heliah was slaughtered along with many of her clan. Under the full moon, the remaining two elders allowed for Apocolieus to feed from them in order to vindicate their losses. As the two elders gave in to death, they chanted of creating a beast that would administer their revenge for all time.

Apocolieus gained incredible strength and abilities; as the story went on, he did indeed vindicate the elders. Though his abilities grew and he became more powerful, he also grew mad with knowledge and the pain of his lost love. Apocolieus lusted for death and the destruction of the human race and, as his kind refused to support him in his quest, they now had become his enemies as well. The story ended with his death, which was a difficult plight, as he had become virtually indestructible. The Gods looked down and began to fear Apocolieus and his power, so they decided to intervene and assist in his demise.

Apocolieus' death was met as the seven Gods had captured him and bound him in silver chains held in place by seven silver daggers. The Gods then caused a nearby volcano to erupt, where they banished him into the molten lava. "Absolute power corrupts absolutely," she thought to herself.

She continued to read on. There were rituals for hibernation, rebirth and other interesting information, but nothing in her section of the book seemed to be helpful for their present situation.

Some of the members began to push their sections of the book back to the center of the table for reassembly as they had completed their reading. Soon, all had completed their tasks, with no results. Lucas stood at the head of the table. "Was there any helpful information found?" Adrian spoke up, "I found nothing to help us with our defense, but there are quite a few rituals and potions here for healing and rebirth, which will be helpful if any of us are injured," she finished.

William chimed in: "There were things that would help, but everything I ran across requires blood or flesh from the opposing force, and we just don't have the time or means to obtain those," he said as he pushed his portion of the book forward.

"Agreed," said Naomi, as she reached for the sections of the book to reassemble it.

Adrian then spoke up out of concern for the book's safety. "Is there somewhere safe that the book can be kept in the case the estate is infiltrated?"

Lucas responded smiling, "Yes, there is a vault below the estate, Naomi will take it there once it has been reassembled," he said as he nodded to Naomi.

"Very good," Adrian responded.

"We seem to have done as much as we can in order to be prepared," Christian said as he looked at Lucas.

"It appears all that is left to do at this point is wait," Lucas added.

The remaining elders began to leave the table and disperse themselves amongst the estate. Only Lucas, Christian and Adrian remained in the Chambers.

"Christian, would you mind locking the doors?" Lucas asked.

Christian looked perplexed, but he nodded and proceeded across the room to secure the chamber doors.

"Ms. Adrian, now that I am fully recovered, I have a debt to settle with you," Lucas began.

"You have no debt to me!" Adrian protested.

Lucas held his hand up to her and began again, "Without you, Christian and I might not be here today. I did not want to make our business the business of Parliament. With the impending conflict approaching, I want you to feed from me in order to enhance your strength, in turn providing better protection for all of us," he continued as he smiled wisely.

Adrian looked to Christian to determine what she should do or say.

Christian, reading the apprehensive expression on her face, replied, "This is a great honor, other than myself, no one amongst our clan has fed on more than one elder."

Adrian nodded as she approached Lucas, "Thank you for honoring me with your gift, I pledge my abilities to the protection of you and our clan," she said as she knelt at Lucas' side.

Christian smiled broadly at her reverence; he gleamed with pride of her accomplishments as he watched on.

Lucas stretched out his arm to her while he placed his free hand upon her head as if it were a crown. "Drink from me," he said as he closed his eyes.

Adrian slowly sank her fangs into his wrist and drank. As his blood began to circulate throughout her body, she began to see his thoughts and memories. She realized within seconds that not only was Lucas sharing his blood with her, but his knowledge and abilities.

Adrian drank her fill and released his arm, her mind a blur as it rapidly processed the newly-gained knowledge and experiences. She remained in a kneeling position, as her physical eyesight had been overtaken by the massive amounts of information that Lucas had funneled to her. After a few moments she was able to regain her composure. She felt as if her physical strength had doubled, perhaps tripled. Her mind was beginning to settle well, as all of the information had seemed to have found its proper place.

Adrian stood and looked into Lucas' eyes, "I had no idea," she said.

"There will be some jealousy from the other elders, as they will know immediately what has happened." None here other than Christian have fed from me and I him," Lucas said. "It is my gift to give, and I have selected you as the recipient" he finished smugly.

"Thank you Lucas," Adrian responded reverently, still distracted by the changes occurring within her body.

"Now, if you two will excuse me, I will need to feed," Lucas said as he stood from his chair in retreat to his suite.

Christian wrapped his arm around Adrian's waist. "How do you feel?" he said, smiling.

"I feel extremely strong physically; mentally, I feel like my mind is processing and filing all of the information that Lucas gave me. It's as if there is this huge energy source inside of me is struggling to find its' place. I just need to figure out how to direct it," she finished.

Christian guided her out of the room and into the hallway. Frederick and William were standing in the directly across from them, both of them immediately looked up in her direction as she entered the sprawling hallway.

Frederick smiled warmly, while William's face turned to a scowl. "I see what Lucas meant," she thought, as she looked to Christian.

"Don't worry about William. He has always owned a weighted sense of self-entitlement," Christian responded mentally.

Adrian smiled at his reassuring thoughts as they continued to make their way to the suite.

William's thoughts were now ringing through her mind: "How could he allow arrogant cunt to feed from him when I have been in his service for centuries?"

Adrian froze in her steps. She felt anger welling up within in her from his comments. She turned and looked directly into his eyes with an intense stare.

Williams face began to flinch in pain as she locked onto his eyes. "In these trying times we do not need conflict amongst us. I suggest that you swallow your pride and direct your focus on our tasks at hand," she growled, as she broke her stare and continued on to their suite.

Christian choked back laughter until they were in the privacy of their room. "I have wanted to put him in his place for a very long time," he said chuckling. "It is just perfect a new female Vampire be the one that finally did," he ended.

Adrian turned and smiled at his comments and reaction, and then began to realize that her stare had caused William physical pain. "Is what just happened normal?" she asked.

Christian smiled and motioned for her to sit next to him on the bed. "There is no normal," he stated, "My abilities were enhanced in different ways from yours," he began. "Feeding from an elder allows for the elder to share his knowledge and enhance your strongest abilities. It is up to you to find out what abilities have been enhanced and how to control the use of them now, I would say that you are well on your way." He smiled as he finished.

Christian sat beside her as she pondered her thoughts. "Let's try something," he said as he continued to observe her. "I want you to move that chair," he said, as he pointed across the room.

Adrian looked at him questioningly and began to stand from the bed.

Christian placed his hand on her leg. "No - from here," he coaxed. "I have a feeling that you can," he added.

Adrian smirked at him and began to focus her attention on the chair. As she stared intently upon it, Christian leaned over and repeated William's rogue thoughts to her. A surge of anger shot through her and the chair flew across the room.

Adrian was astounded by her actions. She turned to Christian with her mouth agape. "I see! If I'm pissed off and stare at something I can throw it across a room!" she said laughingly.

Christian exploded in laughter at her comment. "Something like that," he said, as he stood from the bed and held his arms out to her.

She stood into his warm embrace, "I am so proud of you," he said as he wrapped his arms tightly around her. "Very few newly turned have adjusted as well as you have, even I did not fare so well," he finished.

Adrian melted in his embrace and hoped that the feeling would remain forever as she had vowed to be his mate for eternity. "What shall we do with the remainder of our evening?" she asked.

"I have plans for you for later, however, when all of the elders gather, there is always a banquet which we should be preparing for now," he said smiling. "That reminds me, I have something for you," he said, as he released her from his arms.

He motioned for her to reclaim her seat as he walked into the closet. Moments later he emerged with a large package wrapped elegantly in gold paper with a large red bow on top. "I hope you don't mind, but with everything that has been going on, I sent Sarah and Markus to pick this up for you for this evening," he said, as he sat the box down next to her on the bed.

Adrian smiled with delight as he settled across from her so that he could see her expression upon opening it. She removed the bow and lid from the box then pushed away the tissue paper to reveal a beautiful red silk gown with matching shoes. "Oh, Christian, it's lovely!" she exclaimed, as she stood and held the gown to her.

She ran to the bathroom vanity so that she could admire her reflection. Christian appeared behind her and wrapped his arms around her waist. "There is more," he said, as he lifted a long velvet box that he had hid under the gown.

Adrian turned and accepted the box, which she opened slowly. There staring back at her was a diamond choker with a large heart shaped ruby pendant. She could not believe her eyes.

Christian grinned broadly at her as she gawked at the jewels. "Do you approve?" he asked. Adrian flung her arms around him.

"It is so beautiful, Christian!" she exclaimed as she embraced him.

"I am happy that you like it," he said, as he took the choker from her hands and draped it around her slender neck. He turned her so that she could admire the jewels in her reflection as he fastened it. She giggled with delight as she stared at her at the new sparkling trinket.

"We should get dressed now," Christian said smiling.

Adrian was excited to wear the gown and shoes and, of course, the lovely jeweled choker that Christian had chosen for her. She rushed to undress and change into her new garb. As she slid her feet into the silk shoes, she turned and saw Christian coming from the bathroom donning a tuxedo.

"Oh my God, you look gorgeous!" she exclaimed.

"And you are absolutely breathtaking," Christian said grinning broadly. He walked slowly towards her and kissed her gently on the cheeks then held his arm out to her. "Shall we?" he said eagerly.

Adrian wrapped her arm around his and the two of them made their way to the dining hall. About halfway down the staircase Christian leaned over and whispered in her ear, "I can't wait to see that gown on the floor." Adrian smiled seductively in response.

Chapter Eleven

The banquet had definitely distracted them from what was to come. As they entered the elaborate hall, she saw all of the elders were present and dressed in gowns and tuxedos, their mood had shifted and were now as light as hers and Christian's.

Though the elders all seemed to have dismissed the tense air from earlier that evening, Adrian could still sense an underlying sensation of resentment towards her. She was becoming accustomed to the feeling as she had been an unwanted intruder as a mortal. Most of the elders had warmed up to her, some she feared may never accept the fact that she had been favored by both Christian and Lucas. Her thoughts were soon disturbed as Lucas summoned her and Christian to the head of the table, "This won't help matters at all," she thought to herself.

Christian, sensing the frustration building within her, took her hand and responded silently; "They are a petty brood and quite jealous of you, and rightfully so my beautiful mate." He squeezed her hand reassuringly and leaned to place a kiss on her cheek as they were being led to their seats.

Moments later Christian was seated next to Lucas at the head of the table; Adrian sat proudly next to him. As they settled, he leaned over and to her ear, "The meal will be a little difficult for you to adjust to I'm afraid," he whispered in an odd tone. "This is our tradition; just keep an open mind," he finished as he leaned back into his chair.

Adrian began to wonder what he meant as the servers began to enter the room. Each of the party was served a champagne flute filled with warm blood. Adrian was hesitant to lift the glass to her lips after Christians' warning.

Lucas noticed that she was uncomfortable. "You should drink it before it gets cold," he said, smiling.

Adrian nodded politely, at first she sipped gingerly at the warm thick substance; determining that she enjoyed the flavor, now she, along with everyone else, drained the glass to the bottom.

The servers began to remove the empty glasses from the table and left the room, returning soon after with the appetizers.

Adrian stared at the plate that was set in front of her. It appeared to be some sort of raw liver served on a chilled salad plate. She could see Lucas and Christian chuckling at her as she looked up at them with her jaws agape.

"Just try it, dear," Lucas said as he stifled a smile. "If you do not like it you do not have to eat it, no one will be offended," he said, as he attempted to choke back a laugh.

Adrian continued to sit and stare at the fleshy blob in front of her, and then at the others, who seemed to be enjoying theirs. She lifted her knife and fork and cut a small portion to taste. Surprisingly, she found it tasty. The liver seemed to dissolve in her mouth, leaving a sweet and bloody aftertaste. Before she realized it she had finished her portion. Once the plates were cleared, a large stainless steel table was rolled into the dining hall. Lucas was the first to be served.

The server began to sharpen his knives as his helper drew back a white linen cloth from the table to reveal half of a newly slaughtered bull. "What is your' preference?" the server asked.

Adrian gasped as she looked up to see the half of a slaughtered bull lying on the table behind Lucas. "Oh dear God!" she exclaimed as the room erupted in laughter.

Once the room had settled from her outburst, Lucas placed his order. "I will have a portion of brain with a small slice of kidney."

"And you, sir?" the server asked as he nodded towards Christian. "I will have flesh and a slice of kidney as well."

Adrian summoned the strength to look at Christian's plate; it didn't look as repulsive to her as Lucas' selection. She would order the same when asked by the server.

Once everyone was served, Adrian lifted her fork and knife, taking a deep breath as she began to cut into the blood soaked meat. She found the texture a little difficult to palate but the taste was sweet and made her crave more. The kidney she found quite tasteful as well, soft and chewy with a bittersweet aftertaste, the merlot that she had been served was a perfect complement to its flavor. Once all courses of the banquet had been completed wine and cocktails were served, and the evening droned on, with conversations ranging from centuries past and into the future.

Adrian had grown weary of their company and was ready to retreat to their suite. Christian sensed that she was tiring of the conversation and excused them for the evening, bidding everyone a good night.

Christian and Adrian made their escape up the winding staircase, relieved to leave the group of elders behind for the evening. He slid his hand behind her back and began to unzip her gown before they finished climbing the stairs. She giggled at his advances as she peeked over her shoulder with a seductive glance, encouraging Christian to proceed.

They stopped at the door where he finished removing her gown, throwing it over his left shoulder and her over his right before entering their suite. After kicking the door closed behind them he laid her gently on the bed and stood to admire his prize.

Though she would soon come to know the full potential of her newly acquired strength and abilities, she was still a new vampire, still innocent with lingering mortal flaws. Christian adored her and was consumed with her fascination of her still awakening senses.

Adrian rose up onto her elbows as she beckoned him to come to her. He began to remove his tie and shirt as he leered seductively into her eyes.

She reached out her arms to him, drawing him to her so that she could feel his smooth chest against her naked breasts. Christian softly lay himself atop her as he kissed at her neck. She slid her hands down his muscular torso and began to remove his pants, kicking them to the floor. Christian slid his body down hers, leaving a trail of passionate kisses in his wake.

Adrian gasped as he suddenly sank his fangs into her thigh. Her body pulsed eagerly as he drank from her and then turned his attention to her pulsing vagina. She clutched at the linen comforter beneath her as he sucked lightly at her clitoris. She writhed in ecstasy as he rapidly flicked at her, bringing her to frantic orgasm within moments. Adrian breathlessly called out to him as she crossed her legs tightly over his head.

As her orgasm had ceased, Christian stealthily crawled back over her, hovering just above her face. She wrapped her arms around his neck and kissed him passionately as he sought his way into her.

Christian sighed as he was now completely submerged in her. Eager to gaze into her eyes he rolled them over, leaving her on top of him. Adrian slowly rose and lifted herself onto him; she sped up her pace and then stopped. She began to tease him, allowing only the tip of his penis into her; slowly lowering herself further down upon him with each slow stroke.

Christian clutched at the comforter beneath him as she rotated her hips in a circular motion, stroking him slowly. His throbbing cock began to pulsate within her. She plunged him deeply into her and tightened her vagina around him as he exploded into her.

Christian sat up and wrapped his arms around her waist in order to force her down tightly upon his swollen manhood. Adrian bit into his shoulder as he groaned with his release, which seemed to initiate a second wave of orgasm for him. As she drank from him his panting began to subside and he slowly lowered them back to the bed. She released his shoulder and placed a bloody kiss on his neck as she stroked his hair. She glanced at the nightstand to see the clock displaying 10:25 P.M. as she settled her head upon his chest.

Just as her cheek touched his skin the sirens began to blare outside of the estate. Startled, they both jumped from the bed and ran to the window to raise the shutter and survey the grounds. As they looked toward the front entrance, they saw the guards beginning to draw their weapons as black panel trucks skidded to a stop before the gates. Men dressed in combat attire began to spill from the back of the trucks.

Adrian sensed both human and vampires amongst them, her body filled with adrenaline as she looked to Christian in disbelief. "Not again!" she growled, "Not this fucking time!"

The first rounds of gunfire were discharged by the estate guards; signaling the beginning of the offensive that would surely change the future of the Vampire nation. The enemy clans had managed to attack while most of the elders were present at the estate, history would certainly be altered by the results of this conflict.

Adrian and Christian sped from the window to dress and arm themselves as the shutter clamped back down with a thud.

Chapter Twelve

There was a fierce battle beginning at the main entrance. Adrian strained to see through the heavy smoke-filled air as flashes from gunfire littered the grounds. She could see that there were bodies beginning to accumulate on either side of the gate, yet the enemy just kept coming.

Christian turned to Adrian as he sped away to assist the guards, "Station yourself on the roof!" he shouted to her as he sped away.

Adrian turned and ran back into the estate where security and staff were scurrying about on the main level as the elders were preparing themselves for battle. William and Frederick were just starting up the stairs. Adrian filed in behind them.

"Christian has ordered me to the roof," she said, as she inserted a magazine into her assault rifle.

William smirked at her as she kneeled down beside them.

She could sense a sheer hatred emitting from him as he turned away to survey the grounds. "Get over it asshole," she thought to herself as she looked down to the fighting below.

Adrian could feel something evil in the cold night air as she knelt behind the stone barrier and aimed her weapon. She was now aware of gunfire all about the grounds, and felt that she should also be on the ground level, fighting next to Christian. She looked about and took note of where the elders had positioned themselves.

The guards had formed a line of defense in front of the elders. They stood fearlessly under the light of the full moon as they prepared to join in the battle. Adrian shouldered her weapon and began to pick off the invading human militia as they approached the fences. There was a noticeable increase in the number of weapons firing behind her as the guards defending the rear of the estate were becoming outnumbered. Huge spotlights were criss-crossing the grounds, bodies were beginning to litter the lawn and the invasion was getting closer and closer to the estate.

So far Adrian had only picked humans from the crowd and wondered where the clans were. She could see the elders scattered amongst the guards on the lawns, slicing at the opposing forces as they charged in the direction of the estate. Naomi stood west of the immense water fountain at the front entrance. She had accumulated a large pile of bodies around her. She fought fiercely as the humans charged towards her in groups. Adrian could no longer abide by Christian's wishes; she had decided that she would be of more assistance on the ground. She turned to inform William and Frederick she was leaving them, they were nowhere in sight. Suddenly, her senses began to tingle. Something had her in its sights.

Quickly, she changed out the gun clip from hollow points to silver bullets, then turned to brace her back onto the concrete wall. Just as she had begun to scan her surroundings the one she had come to know as Lazigne landed at her feet.

He stood arrogantly and leered at her with a menacing smile on his lips and vengeance in his eyes. She knew he intended to kill her as a statement to Christian.

Adrian lifted her weapon and aimed at his head "You wouldn't dare, whore!" he laughed.

"Fuck you," she growled as she squeezed the trigger. As the gun discharged, Lazigne pounced. The bullet grazed his left temple. He stood before her and clutched at his smoldering head with his left hand while swatting the rifle from her hands with his right.

Adrian fell back as the rifle flew across the roof. Lazigne pounced again, wrapping his right hand around her neck and lifting her from the ground. "You are Christian's whore, we will see what he thinks once he's discovered that I have fucked you and drank your blood," he growled, his wicked lips curling at her.

"You have made a huge error in judgment by underestimating me, Asshole" she laughed, as she kicked him squarely in his head. She fell to the ground as he staggered backwards as much from her blow as by his shock she had dared to resist him. Lazigne stood erect and steadied himself. Angered by her rebuttal he charged towards her once more, surprised to see that she had risen and was also charging towards him. Adrian ducked at the last moment and turned as he passed her; she jumped onto his back and wrapped her legs tightly around him. She clawed at his face as violently sank her fangs into his shoulder. He, in turn, began to claw at her arms to force her to release him. She knew that she would have to kill him quickly as he was intent on killing her.

Adrian cleared her mind and pushed off of his shoulders, flying over him; then landing behind him. He spun around to face her as she gained her footing.

Now maddened with rage, he slowly walked towards her. "Truly, I have underestimated you" he sneered as he approached. "No matter, I will still fuck Christian's whore before spilling her blood this night" he hissed.

Adrian began to stare into his eyes as fury burned through her. She began to feel a surge of power emitting from within her as she pried into his mind.

Lazigne froze in midstride; the sneer upon his face began to distort into a pain wretched grimace. His skin began to smoke as he released an ear-splitting screech. Adrian leaned over to retrieve the dagger she had placed inside of her boot. Grasping it tightly, she began to walk slowly towards Lazigne, who was clutching his head in agony. She swung the dagger across his neck not once but twice.

Lazigne's knees buckled as he collapsed helplessly at her feet. Adrian pounced on top of him and began to drink his flowing blood as he struggled beneath her. When she had her fill she knelt and forced the dagger into his heart.

"Your blood is putrid and vile with treachery," she said, as she wiped her face and stood. "It seems you are the one that is fucked!" she hissed as she kicked him.

Christian sensed she was in trouble and appeared on the roof next to her.

Adrian hovered over Lazigne and glared into his eyes as he fought for his last breath, "What do you think of Christian's whore now?" she scowled.

Adrian stood to acknowledge Christian just as he drew his sword and took Lazigne's head. Smiling at his handiwork, she leaned to retrieve her dagger, wiping her blade upon Lazigne's frozen chest.

She was exhilarated by her feeding and kill. Lazigne's blood rushed through her filling her with a violent and chaotic urge for battle.

Suddenly, there came a wailing from all around. The remaining members of Lazigne's clan had sensed his demise.

Now even more bloodthirsty for revenge, the opposing clan members became wild in their attack. Adrian glanced down just as Naomi was being attacked by three of the dead lord's clansmen.

"We've got to help her!" she screamed out to Christian. Without hesitation, she leapt from the roof and sped to assist Naomi.

Adrian tackled an elder of the rogue clan and fought fiercely with him. She soon realized hand-to-hand combat offered only limited results, she knew deep within that she was capable of so much more.

Adrian stood motionless for several moments as she summoned the power within her. She began to focus intently into the eyes of her opponent. Within the same moment the elder became rigid with fear as he saw the power welling within her eyes.

Adrian, now remembering that Naomi needed her, reached up and ripped the throat from her victim. She quickly leaned over him as she retrieved her dagger in order to finish removing his head.

Once he had fallen to her feet, she turned her focus onto two other Vampires who were now viciously mauling Naomi to the ground. Adrian became overcame with anger. She sped to Naomi and snatched both of the vampires away from her. With one with each hand and lifted them above her head. She looked down to see Naomi barely clinging to the life that she had in her. She was furious at what they had done. Rage boiled up within her as she lowered the two Vampires to eye level.

She glared at them, they in turn began to tremble with fear as they had never seen such power emit from another of their kind. Adrian clenched her teeth and screamed as something from within her clawed to get out. Her captors went limp in her grip, their frozen faces turning to expressions of horror as their heads burst into flames. Adrian knew that she had caused this. Out of shock, she threw the two burning Vampires to the ground. They landed at Christian's feet just as he arrived.

Christian looked down at her victims as they writhed in pain before directing his baffled gaze to Adrian. He stood staring at her with his jaws agape as she tried to calm the fury within her. Christian had just approached her just as Naomi frantically called out to them.

"Quickly!" she whispered, "You both must feed from me," she said, as she weakly drew her hand to her neck to expose a large gash. Adrian and Christian knelt by her side; they knew that it was too late for Naomi as they held her hands.

"Quickly now!" she managed to whisper again.

Christian and Adrian both leaned to honor her request. As they drank from her, she whispered some barely audible words in a foreign language that Adrian did not understand. When they lifted their heads, she was gone.

Adrian felt something strange coming over her. Her body began to convulse and suddenly she began to levitate against her will. Christian backed away and watched in horror as she was surrounded by a glowing ring of light.

Her convulsions worsened; she was in great pain. She screamed as the pain became unbearable. Her scream became a deafening screech, causing intense pain to all that were within range of her. The battleground had become dormant as friend and foe alike writhed in pain, covering their ears as Adrian wailed.

As her pain began to diminish, Adrian quieted her scream. As suddenly as it had come upon her, it left her. Though the pain had abandoned its relentless grip on her, something else remained; something powerful surged through her body and mind, something that she feared she would not be able to harness.

Adrian continued to float above the ground. She lifted her head to see that the battle had ceased. The grounds lay littered with dead and living alike. The living were still shaking off the effects of her scream as she lowered herself to the ground. She scanned the scene and took note of those that had lost their lives in the attack.

Adrian began to prepare for retribution as the warriors began to rise from their fetal positions and now directed their attention to her. She allowed the fury to boil over once more. She could feel the power within her surging, eager to escape the confines of her body. She raised her hand and focused her gaze on one of Lazigne's clan as he rose, and at once he burst into flames.

No sooner had he stood upright, he dropped to his knees and began to scream, his limbs flailing in agony as the fire consumed him. She directed her focus onto another nearby Vampire and did the same.

Panic began to strike the hearts of the opposing forces; some knelt in horror to her, while others began to flee the estate. Those that fled were quickly picked off by the estate guards as well as the members of Christian and Lucas' clans. Soon, no others remained, with the exception of those that remained on their knees.

Adrian, now calming herself, looked down at Naomi's lifeless remains. She knelt by her side and drew her hand over her eyes to close them. She hung her head and wished Naomi a safe trip and a happy afterlife and then stood.

As she turned, she saw that Lucas and Christian were standing behind her. There was an odd air about them, and obviously some things would need to be discussed after what had just happened. The three of them stood silently staring into one another's faces, none of them knowing quite what to say.

Adrian broke the silence, "Shouldn't we bring Naomi inside?" she asked.

Lucas glanced around Adrian, his eyes settling on his old friend. "Yes," he replied, as he motioned for two nearby guards to remove her from the grounds and take her into the estate.

Ruth soon appeared by their sides and began to look at Adrian with the same expression that Lucas and Christian were wearing. She began to feel apprehensive and a sense of dread welled up inside of her.

Lucas stretched his arm out to her. "Will you join us in the chambers Ms. Adrian? It seems we have some things to discuss" he said as he ushered her back into the estate. .

Chapter Thirteen

The Chambers held a completely different atmosphere for her now. Before the battle, the air had been thick with anxiety as they'd prepared for attack. Though anxiety was still present, it was now blended with heavy dread and fearful whispers as she stood at the sprawling wooden doors.

Adrian proceeded to the center of the room amongst some of the other elders that had already begun to gather. They whispered amongst themselves as they glanced warily up at her. Christian had even seemed to distance himself from her since the incident. She began to feel unwanted and paranoid; perhaps she was overreacting, she thought, as she folded her hands in front of her.

The chamber doors closed with a solid thud behind her. She began to feel that she was now on trial. Lucas stood behind the tall podium at the front of the room. He sighed heavily as he searched for words before speaking.

"In light of the events of this evening, there are some things that need to be discussed in order to protect the clan," he began. "Adrian, come and stand before me," he said.

Lucas wore the expression of a disappointed father as he watched her solemnly approach to stand before the podium.

"Can you explain to me how you came to have these abilities you displayed before us this evening?" he asked.

Her heart sank as the questioning began. "I am not sure what happened" she began. "Naomi asked for Christian and me to feed from her as she was dying. After she passed, I became enraged as I stood mourning her loss, and then something strange began to happen within me" she finished.

"One does not come to possess this type of power from feeding on one elder" Lucas coaxed.

"I see" she said. "I have fed from four elders this evening, three by invitation," she finished defensively.

"Explain" Lucas coaxed further.

Adrian hung her head as she saw that she would now be defending herself to those that she had spent her evening defending. "You yourself invited me to feed upon you early this evening, I fed on Christian in the heat of passion later, I fed on Lazigne as I fought him on the roof, and Naomi bid me as well as Christian to feed from her before her life force faded. Are these the answers that you search for?" she asked as her eyes filled with tears.

"Is there anything that you wish to add?" Lucas prodded.

"The only other thing to add is that when we fed from Naomi, she was saying something in a foreign tongue. I do not know what it meant," she added. "What is it that I have done wrong?" she asked as she fought off the tears that burned at her exhausted eyes.

"That is what we are trying to determine," Lucas answered coldly. "You may leave the chambers while we meet, we will send for you upon our coming to a decision," he stated as he blatantly avoided her stare.

Adrian turned to walk from the chambers. She looked to Christian for support, but he turned his head from her as she faced him and averted his eyes to the floor. She felt lost in the world again. "This cannot be happening," she thought. In one brief moment her life had changed yet again. Her heart mourned, as those that she had trusted now seemed to have abandoned her. "I do not know what I have done to bring this on myself," she thought. "They all seem to suspect me of treachery when I have fought to protect them."

Adrian was numbed as all of them, including Christian as seemingly they had all now turned their backs on her. "At this point, even if I am found innocent, I know I no longer belong here," she thought, "I cannot live amongst those who would turn their backs so quickly on me with no explanation and I certainly can never return to my home now." Adrian sat emptied, filled with heartache as she awaited the chamber doors to open for her once more.

Nearly an hour passed before she was summoned back into the chambers. She stood weakly, as her emotions had drained her physically. Slowly she made her way through the chamber doors. Immediately she looked to Christian to see if he would face her, but he continued to stare forward as she passed to approach the podium.

Lucas stood as she stopped before him. "There is a great shadow of suspicion cast upon you now," he said. "Having read your portion of the book and knowingly feeding from not three but four elders, it seems you may have had an ulterior motive," he finished. "We have no tolerance for those who would pursue their own hidden agendas at the risk of the Clan," he continued.

Adrian began to speak but was immediately silenced. Her heart broke within her; in just a few short hours, she felt that she had now lost everything.

Lucas droned on about her actions but the sound of her world crumbling was louder than his voice. She heard nothing further until he asked, "What do you have to say for your actions?"

Adrian tried desperately to compose herself before speaking, "I did not know that what I was doing was wrong. I am a new Vampire, I had chosen to live my life with Christian as a mortal. I pledged my loyalty to this Clan and risked my life several times as both mortal and vampire in order to protect its members as well as the estate. I resent being in this position, especially for something that was done out of ignorance with no malice intended," she continued. Adrian took a deep breath and finished her thoughts, "Regardless of what you have decided, I cannot be a part of anything where those you trust are so quick to turn their backs on you. I no longer feel like a part of this Clan and I feel that your suspicions of me are unjust and you have shunned me for doing everything that I could to protect us. In just moments I have lost all that I have held dear yet again. I have nothing further to sacrifice and nothing more say," she ended.

She glanced toward Christian once more, who continued to stare at the floor and would not acknowledge her.

Lucas cleared his throat as her words appeared to have made him emotional as well. "As Clan Leader and Head of the Parliament, I have no other choice but to expel you from the confines of the estate for a period of ten years. Parliament has determined you will need to be observed from a distance to determine if you are trustworthy of reclaiming your position within the Clan," he finished.

Adrian was numbed but not shocked by his words. With no desire to remain in their presence, she turned to leave the chambers. Christian was now looking directly at her. He appeared to be saddened by the turn of events, but his grief was no match for hers. She could not understand why he had not stood up for her, why he had remained silent and looked away as she looked to him for support. Whatever the reason, it was now irrelevant to her. She walked from the chambers into the foyer to see that dawn was soon approaching.

She chose to leave the estate immediately, as she assumed that Christian would try to speak with her if she had waited until the next nightfall to leave. Surely the sun's burning rays would bring her less pain than anything he could say to her at this point.

Adrian fled into the remaining darkness and did not stop until she was in the thick of the surrounding forest, where she fell to the ground and began to sob. She could feel Christian trying to pry into her mind. She pushed him away and closed herself off to him. Every inch of her body writhed from the pain of a broken heart. Adrian crawled through the dank and musky soil of the forest floor until she came upon a huge downed hollow tree with a burrow beneath.

She sobbed as she climbed through the rotting trunk, curling herself up into a ball where she would spend the duration of the day covered in rotting mulch.

Adrian cried until she surrendered to exhaustion. When she awoke she was surprised to find that she had slept at all. The sun had barely sunk from the sky as she made her way out of her burrow.

She sat on the cold soil and tried to determine where she would relocate. Should she go home? There wasn't much left there for her, not to mention the fact that Christian would surely look there for her. She stood and began to wander through the forest as she contemplated her next move. She determined she would find her way back to her home in Louisiana, contact one of her Realtor friends and have her home sold. In the meantime she would have no means to support herself. Getting back to her home was the only logical answer there was for her at the moment, though she would first have to find means back into the United States.

As she wandered, Adrian had come to a stream where she leaned down in the moonlight to wash her face. Above her in the still night sky she saw a jet; it appeared to be preparing to land. She knew that if she could find her way to an airport she would be able to sneak into a cargo hold and hitch her way back to the States.

Adrian stood and began to speed in the general direction of the jet. Soon after, she stood at a tree line where just ahead lay a mass of intertwining landing strips. Adrian sped across the landing field and into the terminal.

She appeared briefly in front of the digital displays and found a flight that would be landing in New Orleans. "Perfect," she thought. Having memorized the flight number, she sped to the departure gates and found the jet being prepared for its upcoming flight. The cargo bay was open and was being loaded. Having no better opportunity than now, Adrian slid from the edge of the corridor and in through the conveyor belt, nestling herself against the back wall of the cargo hold just as bags were being thrown in on top of her.

She settled in for a long flight. The cargo hold was cramped and very cold, as cold as the glares of the elders the previous night. Adrian began to cry once more as she thought of Christian and Lucas turning their backs on her. She soon began to feel a different coldness, a cold that was beginning to overtake her thoughts and emotions. Though she was not well versed in the ways of the Vampire, she could not fathom why Christian had done nothing to protect her from the Parliament, she would never lay eyes on him or any of the elders again, she would never find forgiveness for them within her.

Whether his restraint was political or not, she had no compassion for him. She clenched her fists as she remembered the last kiss he had placed on her forehead, the last time they made love, how happy they were. She could feel the pain within her eating away at everything that she was. She felt no more sense of value, no love for life, no more mortality and no reason to be.

Adrian curled up into a ball on the cold metal floor and waited for the plane to land. Hours passed before she felt the plane begin to make its final descent. Having lost all concept of time, she would have to wait and see if she would be able to leave the cargo hold or not once it landed. Soon the plane was taxiing into the gate to unload passengers. She prepared herself for the worst once the doors were opened, but much to her surprise, muggy Louisiana night air filled the hold.

Adrian rushed from the plane and began to transport herself from landmark to landmark until she arrived at her own front gate just before sunrise. Her home was abandoned - no security, no staff, just her, she was relieved to be alone.

She trudged down the driveway to find her front door locked. She reached into the flower bed to retrieve her emergency key and let herself in. Once inside her home she felt a sense of being, though she knew it would be only temporary.

She turned and flipped the switch to lower all of the steel shutters. As they slammed into place she made her way to the kitchen and poured a glass of Christian's wine. Her hands shook as she thought back to sharing meals with him at the very bar she struggled to stand in front of now.

She walked into her office and sat at her computer to email one of her agents about selling the house. In order to avoid a mountain of questions, Adrian lied and said that she and Christian had moved to Grenoble and that she was happy there.

She then made arrangements to have her belongings packed away and moved into storage as she knew that she would not be able to stay at her home. There were too many memories now, as well the possibility of Christian coming there to find her.

Adrian did not sleep this day, as the pain in her heart would not allow it. She spent the day planning, packing and consolidating her accounts. She would prepare to leave once the sun had set so that she could feed. She would not return until just before dawn, as she would want to avoid any chance of being contacted by Christian.

Adrian went to her bedroom and showered the filth from her body then dressed in preparation for the sun to set. She sat quietly as she struggled to dissect the events of the last 24 hours yet she would likely never fathom why Christian and her new found family had immediately turned so coldly on her. Once the skies were dark she reached for her keys and left her home.

Adrian drove through the small town just north of her home in search of a victim, a plan, some sign of what she should do, any answer that she may find. As the hour grew later she found herself on the Interstate still driving north. "Where the hell am I going?" she sighed. She pulled to the shoulder of the road and tried to compose herself. As the car rolled to a stop, she looked up to see an armored truck pass her. Adrian continued to stare at the taillights; she knew that its contents could offer her a new beginning.

Adrian slammed the car in drive and began to follow the truck. She noticed no oncoming traffic and the next exit wasn't for another several miles. She began to drive erratically and passed the truck swerving from lane to lane before slamming on the brakes just ahead of the truck. She opened the car door and fell out onto the cold pavement just as the truck slowed to a stop before hitting her. She could see the silhouettes of two burly security guards through the beams of their headlights as they raced to her side.

"Are you okay, Miss? What happened?" one of them asked, as he reached down to check her pulse.

"Call it in!" he shouted to the other guard as crouched down beside her, still frantically searching for her nonexistent pulse. The second guard fumbled for his radio as he too began to hover over her motionless body.

Adrian, sensing the timing was right, jumped up suddenly and grabbed both guards by their throats. She stared intently into their terrified eyes as she lifted them from their feet.

She carried them to the back of the still idling truck, "Open the door!" she said bluntly as she turned them to face the keypad.

They fumbled for their keys as they dangled from her grip but soon they managed to open the back door. She sat them on the ground behind the truck and stared into their eyes. "You will remember nothing," she said.

Adrian watched on as their eyes glazed over at her command, she could feel their minds surrender to her. She quickly sprang into the back of the truck and grabbed six of the eight bags present, then sped to throw her cargo into the trunk of her car.

She then returned to the truck and ripped the onboard camera from the dash. Before leaving the scene, she returned to the guards in order to issue her last command, "Get into the truck and drive."

The guards nodded then walked obediently to the cab of the truck, which soon was nothing more than taillights fading into the distant horizon.

Adrian turned around in the neutral ground and began to head for home as dawn was now nearing. The increase of early morning traffic kept her on the Interstate longer than she had expected. The sun was burning away the night sky as she pulled to the gate. Her arm smoked as she reached to punch in the gate code. Quickly she sped through the gate and into her garage, closing the door behind her.

Adrian fought off the pain from being exposed to the approaching sunrise and she exited the car to retrieve her haul, which she would hide below in the suite.

She noticed that there had been no sign of anyone having come to look for her as she walked through the main level of the house. "Just as well" she mumbled to herself as she flipped the lever to access the suite.

This being the first time that she had been in the suite since her return, her heart ached as she looked to the bed where she and Christian had made love after he had nursed her back to health. His clothes still hung on the back of the couch.

She dumped the bags of money onto the bed and walked to the couch. Gently, she lifted his shirt and sniffed it. Her eyes filled with tears once more. She could not help herself; she allowed her thoughts to escape her: "Why did you abandon me, Christian?" she cried. She could feel him trying to communicate with her; in her weakened state, it was all she could do to block him out of her head.

She walked to the bed and stared at the canvas bags, then lifted one and ripped it open. Stacks of money fell from the bag.

Soon after she had opened all six of the bags. Her bed was covered with stacks of twenty, fifty and hundred dollar bills, just over eight hundred thousand. She became relieved with the realization she could now relocate.

Still too unsettled to rest, she walked to the computer and began to search for her new home. By noon she had contacted four Realtors in reference to homes that she had found in obscure places on large land parcels, all with basements. Feeling a small sense of accomplishment, she headed upstairs to finish packing her clothes, as she would soon book a flight to go and view the properties.

As she entered her bedroom the house phone rang. She turned to it and stared, knowing that she would not answer. She froze as Christian's voice rang through the answering machine. "Adrian, are you there? Please pick up, you don't understand, there was no time to explain. I had . . ." The recording cut off.

Adrian sank to the floor, "You're right, I don't understand!" she screamed as she sobbed. "You will never hurt me again! No one will!" she screamed as she drew her knees beneath her chin.

She rolled over onto her side and cried until her tears turned to blood. Now weakened, she surrendered herself to sleep once more, laying only feet from where she had lost her mortal life.

Chapter Fourteen

When she awoke it was nearly nightfall. Adrian rushed to load her luggage into her car. Half of the cash from her haul was now placed securely in her closet safe, the other half in her luggage. Before leaving, she scanned the room for what she knew to be the last time she would know it as home.

Adrian rushed to her car to leave. As she backed from the garage, she noticed her cell phone and a red rose lying on the step at the front door. She fought the urge to retrieve her phone as she knew there would be messages there from Christian. She jammed the car in gear and sped to the gate and then onto the rural highway heading towards New Orleans.

Adrian drove to the airport and checked in early for her flight to Memphis, giving her enough time to make arrangements at a hotel near the Memphis Airport; she would be able to check in well before dawn.

By 8:30 she was boarding her flight. As she settled into her seat her mind began to clear from the rushed state that she had been in. She could hear Christian calling for her; she knew that he was in her house. She decided to answer him. "I hear you, now hear me: You have betrayed me, I trusted you and vowed to be loyal to you for eternity while forsaking everything that I had ever known. I loved you with all I was. You have taken everything from me, my past, my present and now my eternity. You will never hurt me again, I will not allow for you to find me and I will never return to my home." Tears poured down her face as she sent her message to him. She could feel him weeping as her words lashed out at him.

Christian fell to his knees, as he had indeed heard her message. He buried his head into the bed they had made love in; he knew she meant what she said. He also knew she was powerful enough to cloak herself wherever she was, making it impossible for him to ever find her again. He wept as he felt her push him out of her mind, knowing he would never see her again.

As Adrian's flight took off for Memphis, Christian's blood boiled at the Parliament for having tied his hands while they made such a rash decision as expelling her from the clan. What she did not know was that he too had been expelled, as he had been tried after Adrian had fled the estate.

The Parliament worked in strange ways, the old ways, which made it imperative for Christian not to communicate with her prior to trial. Any inclination that the other elders would have made in them having conspired against the clan together would have been viewed as treasonous and would have resulted in their death.

By Christian remaining silent and her fleeing the estate, they were sentenced as lightly as possible in the eyes of their law, by means of expulsion. The elders had such a fear of the legend of Apocolieus that their judgment against him and Adrian had been flawed. Though the decision had not been unanimous, with Parliament, majority ruled.

Christian staggered to his feet, now lost without her for another eternity. He vowed he would never give up searching for her. He would call a meeting with the Parliament to have them reconsider their sentences. Christian turned and looked around the suite once more, remembering how happy Adrian and he had been there. He, now a broken Vampire, left the house determined to fight for what he was not willing to lose twice within his lifetime.

Chapter Fifteen

The plane now skidded to a stop. Adrian prepared to disembark the cabin. She felt completely lost as she followed the crowd of passengers to the baggage claim area, the sounds of their beating hearts echoed through her emptiness, agitating her further.

Now nearly driven mad by their aroma, she fought to maintain her composure and blend in to her surroundings. Yet their heartbeats continued to echo in her head along with their petty thoughts until it was deafening. She had not been in a crowd since she had been turned; she found she was unprepared for the situation.

Adrian was becoming frustrated and now rushed for time. In her anxiety her fangs began to protrude. Thankfully her bags appeared on the conveyor, allowing her to leave the terminal quickly and without being noticed.

Once outside the airport, she summoned a taxi to take her to a hotel, where she had requested a room with no windows.

Adrian, now settling into her room, lay down on the bed and began to mourn the loss of her life. As tears stung her eyes once more, her anger grew towards the elders. She felt that if she were to approach them and discuss the matter in more detail it would easily be resolved. However, their lack of trust in her after everything she had done for them only told her their true nature had been revealed. Now that they had turned their backs on her, she had no trust or remorse for them. "They will have to fend for themselves the next time there is a threat against their clan," she thought to herself. Out of sheer exhaustion, Adrian finally fell asleep, not to awaken until the following evening.

Christian, now waking at his New Orleans estate, tried to focus on Adrian and her location within his first waking moments. He could only gather flashes of where she had been. Now he knew that she had been on a flight, but was unable to tell where she had landed or what her purpose had been in going there. "I cannot live this way" he sighed as he stood from his bed.

Christian decided to call Lucas and discuss the situation with him further. "Good evening" Lucas tolled, as he answered his phone.

"Lucas, it's Christian," he muttered. Lucas immediately felt Christian was in much pain.

"You, my friend, are in a bad way, are you not?" he responded.

"I am," Christian muttered. "I am calling to ask that the Parliament reconsider their decision to expel Adrian and myself from the Clan," he continued.

Lucas sighed, he knew his friend was crushed, but the Parliament was stubborn and closed-minded to such things as these.

Christian began to explain the situation in detail with Lucas. He ended by alerting him Adrian had disappeared and would not allow communication between the two of them.

Lucas seemed to be aware of all of the current happenings and agreed with Christian the decision had been a rash one; however, he would have much difficulty in attempting to have the Parliament agree to meet on the topic again.

Lucas ended the conversation with a promise to Christian he would find a way to have the Parliament reevaluate the situation.

Christian sat the phone down and ran his fingers through his hair. Now holding his head, he wept once more for the pain Adrian had been subjected to. He had to find her. There had to be a way.

Adrian had spent her evening looking at homes in the obscure mountains of Tennessee. She had chosen a large ranch style home built on the side of a mountain near a stream that wound through the property. She signed the paperwork and made arrangements for her belongings to be packed and shipped to her. She would return to her home only once more to retrieve the contents of her safe. Adrian returned to her hotel room to book a flight to New Orleans for the last time. .

Chapter Sixteen

Several days later she found herself settling into her new home, her belongings lay scattered around the new house in carefully packed and labeled boxes.

Adrian was withering away, merely a shell of who she once was. She had not fed and had found very little sleep. Her broken heart was her only motivation. Her mind would not let go of memories of her time with Christian. "This was just so wrong!" she thought to herself. She knew she could not survive more heartbreak, mentally or physically. She continued to wander about the new house, unpacking and rearranging things as she came to them. With dawn approaching, Adrian would soon retire to the basement and finish her unpacking there, though she had had steel shutters installed prior to her moving, giving her freedom to wander the house at all hours.

Meanwhile, Christian mirrored Adrian as he wandered the halls of his New Orleans estate. He had not slept or fed in the past week either as his broken heart taunted him to give up his life. Markus approached him as he sat quietly on the couch.

"Shall we go out this evening?" he gently prodded.

"No, Markus, I have no desire to leave the estate," Christian responded.

"You must feed Lord," Markus nervously coaxed.

Christian stood to his feet and lashed out at Markus, "I have no desire to feed, I have no desire to be!" he growled.

Markus bowed his head and chose his next words carefully, "Surely she will change her mind and what condition will she find you in when she returns? You must feed and keep your strength up for that day." Markus sternly finished.

Christian sighed as he turned to the wall away from Markus. "I suppose that there is some truth in what you say," he surrendered. Christian droningly followed Markus to the car in search of a victim to feed on.

Markus sped his pace in order to open the car door for Christian who nodded politely at his gesture. As he climbed into the back seat he looked down and saw Adrian's lipstick-stained wine glass. His heart sank as he stared down at it.

Christian reached to retrieve the glass and sniffed at it in hopes of finding her scent. Closing his eyes, he inhaled deeply and then saw a brief glimpse of her. He knew that she was in as much pain as he. He hung his head in sorrow as the vision of her disappeared; he gently sat the wine glass back into its holder as he tried to shake her from his mind for just long enough to focus on feeding.

Adrian worked throughout the day turning the basement into her personal suite as the contractors above her worked feverishly to finish improvements before the end of the day. Satisfied with her new living space, she sat on the corner of her bed as she realized the noise from the construction crew had vanished. It was nearly sundown and she now was free to roam the upper levels in their absence.

She knew once the sun had set she would have to feed this night. She decided to drive into town in search of a victim. She had planned to feed quickly in order to return home early that evening to complete unpacking the main level of the house. Once dressed, she made her way out and was in search of prey.

Adrian found her way to the next small town and drove through the tourist-lined streets. She could choose her victim easily from the crowd; but the last lingering particles of her human nature, which she desperately still clung to, would not allow for her to kill indiscriminately. She decided to park and walk through the streets in search of someone more deserving of an ill fate.

As the hour grew later, she walked the darkened back streets where the tourists did not go. Her attention was suddenly drawn as a man screamed out in anger; it seemed he was just a few blocks away from where she now stood.

Adrian ducked through the shadows in search of the commotion. She sensed two heartbeats in an alley to her left. Adrian walked slowly towards the still ranting man. She peered around the corner to see a large man yelling at a young girl.

Suddenly, he drew his fist back and punched the girl in her face. Her frail body crumpled to the ground yet the man began to kick at her as he continued cursing her.

Adrian flew up behind the man and spoke, startling him: "Do you feel like a big man now?" she taunted. The monster of a man spun around to see who had witnessed his actions.

His mouth twisted into a grimace as he turned to face Adrian. He began to leer at her, "Why, do you want to be next bitch?" he said, laughing as he ogled her.

Adrian looked down at the young girl and then back up at the man, "You are next!" she growled as she exposed her fangs to him. She snatched the man by his throat and lifted him from the ground as her fierce eyes reflected the dim street light above them. His face changed from a grimace to an expression of sheer horror.

Adrian slammed him backwards into a brick wall and sank her fangs into his neck as he slid to the ground. She drained him completely and threw his body into a nearby dumpster. "Bitch!" she hissed as she turned to walk away.

Adrian wiped her mouth as she turned to leave then spotted the girl still unconscious on the ground. She realized more harm may come to the young girl if she were left there. She sighed as she lifted her limp body up into her arms and sped away with her.

Adrian darted through the back streets until she found a police car parked outside of a nearby all-night diner. She gently laid the girl across the hood of the car and disappeared into the thin night air.

Having returned to her car, she would now retreat to her new home on the mountainside. For the remainder of the evening she would begin to devise a better plan for her feedings, much like what she had done back home in Louisiana.

As she drove up the narrow and winding mountain road something caught her eye just ahead. There was a wolf in the road that had been struck by another vehicle. Hovering around her were two pups that could have only been a few weeks old. Adrian stopped the car as she realized she could not leave them alone in the world to starve.

She stood from the car and walked over to the pups, which were too frightened to run. Gently she stooped and held her hands out to them, "Come to me," she whispered, as she looked into their desperate eyes. The pups stood and walked weakly to her; it was apparent they had not been walking for long. Adrian lifted them into her arms and returned to her car, she held them snugly against her chest as she drove back to her new home.

Once inside, she released them onto the floor near the fireplace and went to the kitchen to find something to feed them. As she turned she saw that they had followed her. They both sat obediently and watched her as she moved about the kitchen. A male and a female, she would name them Sheba and Caesar, she thought as she put a pack of ground meat into the microwave to thaw and filled a bowl for water for them. As she sat the bowl on the ground they continued to watch her, still seated in the same spot. Adrian looked at them questioningly. "Drink," she said.

The pups stood and walked to the bowl then began to lap at the cool water. Soon after, the timer of the microwave tolled that the meat had been defrosted. She opened the package and broke the meat up into another bowl and placed it down next to the water. "Eat," she said, as the pups looked up at her. They seemed to understand her commands. "This will make housebreaking much easier!" she chuckled.

The pups were a welcomed distraction to her. She would spend a great deal of time training them to be her protectors. Adrian left the pups alone as they ate, she retired to the living room in search of local news; she would use the same tools as before to find her prey. "Let's see what kind of scum the State of Tennessee has to offer," she mumbled as she flipped through the channels.

She settled on a local channel just as the pups had come to sit at her feet. "Come" she said, as she patted the seat next to her. The female attempted to climb up to her first. Adrian smiled as the pup struggled. She leaned over and lifted her to her face. "You are Sheba," she said as she kissed the pup on her head and sat her down beside her. The male sat whining at her feet; she lifted him up to her face as well. "You are Caesar" she said as she kissed him on the head as well, setting him down next to his sibling. The pups settled in next to her and with full bellies were soon off for a long nap.

Adrian returned her attention to the local news channel and began to make notes on several different cases and wanted suspects. She sat back into the couch and thought, "If I am to survive, I need a purpose. Taking criminals off of the street is a good one, but perhaps I should consider this on a larger scale."

Adrian reached for her laptop and typed into the search bar, *FBI Most Wanted List.* Once on the FBI website, she noted all of the wanted suspects had rewards on their heads. "An honest way to make a living," she thought aloud.

She would spend the remainder of the evening researching the policies and procedures but would put more thought into it on the following day.

Now exhausted, she decided to retire before dawn. As she stood from the couch, she looked down to see the pups now stirring. She lifted them to her and carried them to the front door. "You will go do your business now and return to me immediately," she said as she set them on the ground.

She watched intently as the pups wandered into the tree line. She could sense that they had not gone far; a few minutes later they returned to her feet. "Very good!" she said, as she lifted them from the ground to take them with her into the basement suite. She and the pups would settle in for a long sleep.

Now having some sense of purpose, she closed her eyes as she settled into bed. Though she was distracted with the research that she would have to do in the next few days, Christian's face was the first thing that came to her mind.

She knew that he was suffering with her. She could feel him mourning her. She rolled over in the bed attempting to push him from her mind, but to no avail. Nearly an hour had passed while she fought with her thoughts. Adrian sat upright in the bed and rubbed her face with her hands. She knew he would not stop calling for her; she knew he would be searching for her and eventually, as he had turned her, he would find her. "Why is everything so fucked up?" she sighed.

She could see Christian lying on his side in the bed, his face streaked with tears. He was awake as well and she could sense his thoughts were on her. She began to think of what she would do if he were to appear at her door one day. Her first thought was to reach out and hold him. She shook her head at herself. "I still love him" she said aloud. "How can I love him when I can't trust him? He turned his back on me and allowed this to happen without a word, not even a glance! What the fuck is wrong with me?"

Adrian slung herself back down into the bed, crossing her arms over her face. She needed to know why; she needed answers but was not sure that she was ready for them. Adrian's mind exhausted her with endless unanswered questions but eventually sleep did come.

Christian, however, found little sleep, if any. His blood still boiled within him, his thoughts had turned vengeful now. It had been over a week since he spoke with Lucas about having his and Adrian's sentence lifted, with no response. "I formed this Parliament! How dare they disrespect me this way!" he fumed.

They, after all, were the root of his misery. Lucas had been his ally for centuries. "How could he turn his back on me this way?" he thought, as he paced the halls. "They have caused me to lose my soul mate for the second time in my long and wretched life!" he screamed. Christian turned to a nearby marble table and rammed his fists through it, sending shards of wood and marble flying down the corridor. He stood staring blankly at the pile of rubble before him, his fists still clenched in grief. Christian grew even more furious. He turned and stormed down the hall to encounter Markus and Sarah, who had come to investigate the loud crash.

"Lord, what has happened, are you alright?" Sarah panted as she approached him.

"No! I am not alright! Markus, have the pilot ready the plane for takeoff, we are leaving for Grenoble immediately!" he scowled as he continued to charge his way down the long marble hallway. His voice echoed throughout the estate. "I have had my fill of this!" he growled as he made his way to his suite to pack a bag.

Markus appeared as his door, "Lord, if I may; if you go to Grenoble now, you will end any hopes of them reconsidering their sentence," he warned.

Christian froze, then slowly turned to Markus, "Fuck the Parliament and their rules, they will reverse their decision or else!" he growled.

Markus hung his head and stepped back through the doorway. "Perhaps I may suggest that you call ahead before going," he mumbled.

Christian, becoming even more irritated, bared his fangs at Markus and hissed wildly. Never in all of the years of service had he threatened Markus.

Christian's heart sank as Markus turned to retreat down the hall. He sat on the corner of his bed and wrung his head through his hands. As he lifted his head, across the room he spotted something under the chair that sat in front of the fireplace. He stooped to retrieve what he found to be one of Adrian's red silk shoes. He sunk into the chair and placed the shoe in his lap. "I cannot lose you" he whispered.

He stood and placed the shoe in the chair before continuing to pack. "Surely if I can speak with them face-to-face they will change their minds," he thought as he threw the last of his clothes into the bag. Christian stormed from his suite and was met by Markus awaiting him with the car. Markus drove in silence to the hangar, still shaken from Christians' threatening behavior towards him earlier.

Markus pulled the car up to the plane and exited the car to retrieve their luggage but Christian was already walking towards the plane. Within moments, they had boarded the craft and the pilot was preparing for takeoff.

Chapter Seventeen

Adrian had spent the last several days researching policies and laws associated with bounty hunting as well as researching the *FBI's Most Wanted List* for fugitives. Several stood out to her as she did her research. She felt she could locate at least four of them and retrieve them quickly. One of them in particular she felt would be an easy nab.

Aaron Joseph Brown was wanted for computer fraud and embezzling. He looked like a computer nerd, definitely a non-violent. His background showed he had family in Phoenix, Arizona. Adrian could now see the house where he was living. There was a $300,000.00 reward for him. All of these criteria made his capture more attractive to her.

The idea sat well with her, so she began to compile any data she could find on Brown and believed she had confined her search to one small outlying area of Arizona. Several hours later, Adrian decided she would definitely pursue Brown. She stacked all of her research into a folder, closed her laptop and booked a flight out for that night.

Adrian watched from the window of the plane as it began its final descent. She sensed the area Brown had been hiding in as the landing strip came into sight in the distance. She smiled, as she could see him sitting at a computer in a small room near the front of a light blue house. It was as if she were standing there behind him, just as the others before him.

She hurried to disembark the plane to rent a car and check into her hotel room with intentions of retrieving Brown before morning. Adrian rushed to check in and confirm that her room had no windows; once satisfied, she left the hotel with several hours of darkness to spare.

Driving north from the hotel, she left the lights of the city behind her. Soon she approached a rural area and began to sense that she was closing in on Brown's location. She turned down a narrow paved road and was immediately drawn to the blue house she had envisioned earlier. She felt a pressure building within her, her instincts taking over as she pulled in front of the house and turned on the hazard lights. She sat for a moment while collecting her thoughts, then decided on a plan.

Adrian climbed from the minivan and walked to the front door. She had barely knocked when Brown opened the door.

"I'm so sorry to bother you, but my car just died and my cell phone won't let me call out. Do you have a phone I could use?" she asked while turning on her charm.

Brown smiled at the beautiful woman standing before him. "Sure, I'll take a look at your car for you too," he smiled as he stumbled over himself to help her.

"Could you show me to your phone - and maybe to the bathroom?" she asked shyly.

"Oh, sure," Brown replied. "This way" he said, as he motioned for her to enter. Adrian felt as if she had walked into a brick wall as she tried to enter. She had forgotten she needed a formal invitation.

Quick to react, she called behind him, "You know, I'm being such an inconvenience, I'm so sorry to have disturbed you at this hour. You have been so kind, are you sure I can come in?" she asked.

"Oh, please come in, you've been no problem," he said.

Adrian grinned as she walked through the door, closing it behind her as she called out his name. "Aaron" she tolled melodically.

The man froze in his steps, "I didn't tell you my name," he said as he turned slowly to face her.

Adrian appeared in front of him immediately and stared intently into his eyes. She could feel herself taking over his thoughts. "You want to come with me." Nothing will stop you from coming with me. You want to obey my every command. There is nothing that satisfies you more than to be at my beckoned call, do you understand Aaron?" she asked.

Brown slowly nodded his head. His eyes were glazed over; he was now in a deep trance. Adrian smiled and decided to test her hold on him.

"Aaron, I want you to fix me a glass of water with four ice cubes, hurry and bring it back to me."

Brown fled to the kitchen and quickly returned with her order, obediently holding the glass up to her.

Adrian glanced for long enough to count 4 ice cubes, "You drink it," she said.

Brown drank the glass dry and stood waiting for his next order.

"Close your laptop, grab your wallet, and come with me," she ordered.

Brown quickly obeyed her orders and followed her to the van.

"Get in," she said, as she motioned to the passenger door.

Brown, now buckled into the seat next to her, stared blankly through the windshield. Adrian laughed aloud. "Piece of cake!" she said under her breath, as she started the engine.

Soon they were on their way to the U. S. Marshall's office in Phoenix, less than twenty miles away. Adrian dialed the number ahead of her arrival. She turned to Brown as the line began to ring. "Sleep," she ordered. Brown's head dropped as he fell into a deep sleep.

"U.S. Marshall's office" the voice grunted on the other end of the line. "Who is in charge there tonight? Captain Jameson," he huffed. "I need to speak with Captain Jameson then," she replied. She could hear her call being transferred; soon after, there was an answer.

"Captain Jameson here, how can I help you this evening?" he tolled.

"My name is Adrian . . . Fury, I'm a bounty hunter from Tennessee. I am bringing in Aaron Joseph Brown; he is in my custody. I will deliver him to you within the next ten minutes, providing that there is a check in the amount of $300,000.00, his reward, waiting for me." she finished.

"Ma'am, did I understand you correctly?" he asked.

"Yes, you did, now in nine minutes I will be at your front door" she stated firmly.

"Yes, Ma'am, I will be there waiting for you," he said, as he hung up the phone.

Nine minutes later she arrived at the complex where a middle-aged Captain Jameson stood waiting with two other deputies.

Adrian climbed from the van and walked around to meet them, "Check made to "Cash," she said, smiling. "Policy prohibits . . ." Captain Jameson began. Adrian raised her hand to him and glared into his eyes, then at the two deputies beside him. She turned her gaze back to Jameson, "You want to write the check out to 'Cash' and you want to do that right now!" she ordered.

Jameson turned and sped through the doors. "Bring the check and all of the paperwork back to me immediately," she called behind him. Minutes later, she was signing all of the necessary forms, "Adrian Fury." With all documents executed, she removed the Captain and his deputies from her spell.

"Pleasure doing business with you, Captain," she smiled, as she held her hand out to him. Stunned, the Captain shook her hand and looked down to see his paperwork completed.

"I have something for you," she said as she turned and opened the side door of the van. She retrieved the laptop and wallet and handed them to Captain Jameson as she shouted "Wake!" over her shoulder.

Brown woke and looked to her for his next order. "Come out of the van with your hands in front of you, walk to the deputies and allow them to cuff you," she said.

Captain Jameson and the deputies wore a baffled expression upon their faces as they looked back and forth at each other.

"I hypnotized him," Adrian laughed, as she could see their questioning expressions.

"No shit?" Jameson asked, as the deputies escorted Brown through the doors.

"Hold up a minute," Adrian called behind them, "Aaron," she called out.

The deputies allowed Brown to turn and look at her. "You are released," she said.

The haze disappeared from Brown's eyes as he realized that he was in custody and had no idea how he had gotten there. "What the fuck!" he screamed, as they dragged him into the building.

"Have a good evening Captain," she tolled as she walked back to her van.

Jameson waved as he rushed into the building to start the booking process.

Adrian arrived back at the hotel shortly afterward and prepared for a long rest, content with having accomplished her mission.

Christian was now arriving at the Grenoble estate, his jet taxiing its way into the hangar. With two hours of sunlight left he would have to wait inside the jet until the sky turned dark.

Everywhere he looked around the cabin he was reminded of her; he wandered back into the master suite. As he sat on the edge of the bed, he remembered a token of hers that he had placed in the bedside drawer. He slid the drawer open and retrieved her black lace bra. He thought back of the encounter when he had sliced the bra off of her the night before Parliament had blessed their union. He hung his head as he fought back the recurring tears, "Fucking hypocritical bastards!" he growled as he sniffed her scent from the bra. He laid across the bed and clutched the lace token to his chest as his blood lusted for justice.

His mind was a blur and his frustrations grew. Time could not pass quickly enough before he would have his face-to-face with Lucas. He had waited long enough! Christian called for Markus.

"Yes, Lord," he answered as he made his way to Christian.

"Markus, first I want to apologize for my actions earlier, I am sorry I lost my patience with you. You have been a loyal servant and I will not forget that again," he ended.

"I understand the pressure that you are under sir, have no worry, I will not leave your side through these difficult times," he responded.

"I am relieved to hear that, thank you Markus. Now I need you to bring the car around."

"But Lord, the sun has not completely set" Markus stammered.

"I understand," Christian responded, "I have grown weary of waiting," he finished.

"Yes, Lord," Markus begrudgingly answered as he turned to go retrieve a car.

Christian waited until he heard the car pull into the hangar. He rushed from the jet and ducked into the car as Markus slammed the door behind him. Markus climbed behind the wheel and looked back at Christian, "Are you sure you won't wait just an hour more?" he pleaded.

"I'll be fine, thank you for your concern. Just get me there quickly," he said as he lay down in the seat and covered himself with his jacket.

Markus sped to the front entrance of the estate and was met by Security, who had been alerted of their presence once the car had left the hangar. The shutter rose from the front entrance as Markus slid the car to a stop and raced to assist Christian make his entry.

His skin sizzled as he climbed from the car; Security raced to him, covered him with a blanket and rushed him inside just as the shutters slammed shut behind them. Christian's skin cracked as it continued to smolder. His knees buckled in pain as Markus removed the blanket and helped him to a chaise within the entryway of the foyer.

"What is this commotion?" Lucas demanded as he came from his study to investigate. "Christian! What have you done? Why are you here?" he demanded. "Do you know what you have done?" Lucas stood, jaws agape, as his voice rang through the estate.

Christian staggered to his feet. "I had to speak with you face to face. This has to stop!" he grunted as he choked back the pain.

"To my study!" Lucas ordered, as he pointed down the corridor. Christian trudged into Lucas' study still smoldering from having exposed himself to daylight.

Lucas slammed the door behind them as they entered, "Your very presence here is contemptuous!" Lucas shouted.

"I understand," Christian replied, "However, I am here to plead our case with you," he continued. "None of the events that night were premeditated, I assure you. Adrian has disappeared, I see only glimpses of her, as she has blocked me from communicating with her. Her heart is broken. All she understands is she was abandoned by me as well as her Clan. She doesn't understand why," he pleaded.

Lucas sighed as he sat behind his desk. "You know the laws state Parliament is to have no contact with you, yet you appear here to convince us we have made the wrong judgment. The elders will be furious when they hear of this," Lucas added.

"Lucas! Need I remind you I formed this Parliament? I created law and order throughout the clans. I have asked for no leniency at any point until now. I want this judgment annulled, I will not lose her! I will find her with or without your blessings; if it be without, I will turn my back on all of you. Make your decision now," Christian demanded.

Lucas' jaw tightened at Christian's demands. He stood from behind his desk and glared into Christian's eyes. "Consider yourself an enemy of the Parliament," he growled.

Christian took a step forward and leaned over his desk. "Let me remind you that you are housed in my personal property. You will evacuate immediately as you are now trespassing. Anyone found here the following evening will meet their death," he growled back as he turned and stomped from the study.

Christian charged through the foyer and out the front entrance. Healed from his previous exposure, he was relieved to see that the sun had set. "Drive," he said as he climbed into the back seat of the car.

Markus put the car in gear and drove through the front entrance of the estate. He looked into the rearview mirror to see Christian holding his head in his hands.

Christian could feel Markus staring at him. "I have evicted the Parliament from my property. They have turned their backs on me, I now consider them my enemies," he said as he settled back into his seat. "Take us to the club," he said, as he stared blankly out of the window.

Christian spent the evening and the following day at the club, feeding and preparing for what might come the following night if the elders had not left his estate. He now, drunken with blood and vengeance, had turned cold and vicious once more.

Chapter Eighteen

Adrian had boarded her return flight to Tennessee. She sat quietly in her seat and stared at the check she collected for Brown's reward. She devised a plan to cash the check in order to protect her identity. She would have to obtain identification in the name of Adrian Fury to prevent leaving a paper trail. This necessity would demand that the next fugitive she sought would have to have the abilities to create such documents. Adrian smiled as she folded the check and put it back into her pocket. She felt a feeling of accomplishment that somehow helped to ease the pain of her recent loss.

Upon landing, before returning to her home, she would attempt to find means of cashing the check. With no banks open at night, she knew that she would have to find a gambling venue to complete her mission. Adrian, now back in her car, searched on her navigation system and found Southland Greyhound Park. "Perfect!" she thought. She headed home to check on her pups; she would venture to Southland early the next evening with a well thought out plan.

The two pups sat obediently at the front door as they sensed her arrival. "Hello, Sheba and Caesar" she said as she opened the door. The pups were excited to see her. She closed the door as she lowered her bag to the floor and lifted them to her chest. "I missed you, too" she said. Adrian carried them to the kitchen to refill their food bowls, and poured herself a glass of wine to celebrate her accomplishment.

Her thoughts went to Christian, who she sensed had become volatile. She strained to locate him and realized that he was in Grenoble. "This will not end well" she sighed.

Adrian sat at the bar and considered calling on Lucas to perhaps smooth over his rash behavior. She determined it best to leave the situation alone as Christian, after all, was higher ranking than the Parliament itself. No matter how she fought it, her heart ached for him and she knew that he felt the same. She knew that he would lash out at the elders and also she knew that it was in her best interest not to be involved.

Adrian refilled her glass and wandered into the living room. She sank into the couch and called for the pups to join her. She giggled at them as they strained to find a way up onto the couch next to her. Smiling, she leaned over and lifted them one by one to sit by her. "My babies," she said as she watched them curl up onto one another. Adrian smiled as she stroked their heads; their eyes became heavy and within moments they were swept off to sleep.

She finished her wine as she sat and admired the pups, she then stood and scooped them up to carry them off to bed with her.

Adrian tossed and turned most of the night knowing that Christian was plotting against the elders. Part of her wanted to cry out to him; the other part of her was still numbed by the pain that he had inflicted upon her. Eventually, when sleep took over her thoughts, she dreamed of him and happier days that they had spent together. She could feel him in her arms, his fingers stroking her tousled hair.

The following evening, when the sun had sunk low in the sky, Adrian awoke and began to dress for her mission to have the check cashed and not have her identity discovered. She looked into the mirror before leaving; she wondered how she could look as though all was well all while she was nearly as volatile as Christian.

Adrian reached for her keys and left the house, headed for Southland Greyhound Park.

She arrived shortly after 8:00 to a crowded parking lot. Such a crowd would make it easy for her to remain inconspicuous. She made her way across the main lobby as she blended in with a large group of tourists. After darting through the crowd she approached the customer service desk where she found herself staring into a bubbly round black woman's eyes. "Bring the General Manager to me," she smiled.

The woman nodded oddly, then turned to retrieve the manager. Shortly, she arrived back at the desk, ushering an older, heavyset balding man to the counter. The man smiled as he approached.

"How can I help you this evening, Miss?" he grinned broadly.

Adrian looked intently into his eyes, "You will cash this check for me," she demanded.

"Will I, now?" the man replied chuckling.

Adrian was both surprised and confused by his response; he had not fallen under her control as all of the others had. She slowly reached up and removed the dark glasses from her face. She peered into the man's eyes and suddenly was struck with the realization he was Vampire. The man nodded as her facial expression told him she was aware.

"Come with me," he said as he smiled and motioned for her to follow.

Adrian followed the man into his lush office where he introduced himself only as Vincent before inquiring of her origins.

She knew he did not mean her mortal background; she was hesitant to respond but felt there would be no use in attempting to keep the truth from him.

"Lord Christian turned me, until recently I was a member of his Clan," she volunteered. Vincent nodded. "Christian is a noble Lord," he responded. "I sense much turmoil with you, for what reason have you been separated from your clan?" he asked as he slowly lowered himself into his chair.

Adrian sighed before responding, "The short of it is he chose the wishes of Parliament over me."

"Ah, The Parliament, say no more; those pompous relics have caused me more than a little heartache of my own," he chuckled. So, tell me about this check," he inquired, as he motioned for Adrian to have a seat.

Adrian feeling a bit more at ease, sat across the desk from him and began to explain. "It is from the U. S. Marshall's office, it is legitimate," she began. "This check is a reward for a fugitive named Aaron Joseph Brown," she stated. "I have recently taken up bounty hunting as a way to remain invisible and still legally support myself."

Vincent nodded again. "Interesting but brilliant choice," he said. "Let's have a look at it." Adrian produced the check and laid it on the desk in front of him.

Vincent smiled as he retrieved it and walked to a nearby safe. He returned with several bundles of cash and laid them before her. "You are new to the area," he smiled warmly. "As we share the same bloodline, I am drawn to assist you in any way you may deem necessary," he added as he sat back into his chair.

Adrian smiled and leaned forward, "Then I assume you will have no problem keeping my presence here between the two of us?" she asked.

Vincent sat back in his chair and looked into her eyes, searching for the reason behind the turmoil in her eyes. "Christian was more than your maker, he was your mate wasn't he?"

Adrian hung her head, she had not expected to be confronted with the reminder of the pain that she had struggled to bury deep within. She looked back at Vincent and responded, "Lucas and the others have caused great damage to our relationship, we have both sacrificed so much in their behalf, I am afraid there is no more to give," she said as she fought back tears.

Vincent sat nodding, "I understand, your secret is safe with me. Is there anything that I can do to help you be more comfortable in your new surroundings?" he asked.

"As a matter of fact, there is something I need," she answered as she wiped the tears from her eyes. "I need to create an alias; I need documentation and identification in the name of Adrian Fury," she finished.

Vincent drew his hand to his chin and propped his face upon it. "That can be arranged," he said, after careful consideration. He opened his desk drawer and retrieved a business card, flipped it over and wrote a name and number on the back, then offered it to Adrian. "This gentleman can help you. He is Vampire as well. I will contact him and tell him to be expecting your call," he said smiling warmly.

Adrian stood and gathered the cash, thanked Vincent for his kindness, and offered a favor to him if he should ever need her as thanks in return for his assistance.

"That will not be necessary," Vincent replied, "Our kind has to stick together," he finished, as he stood to escort her to the door. Adrian shook his hand once more as she departed the racetrack and returned to her car.

Her evening had gone much easier than she had expected even though she had been surprised by encountering another Vampire. Adrian now slid into her car and headed for home. She would stop for some brief shopping before her return home, as the pups would require supplies.

Christian, now arriving back at his Grenoble estate, noticed a great deal of activity around the grounds. Instead of the gate opening for him, guards were filing in and blocking the gate. Christian hung his head as he realized the evening would go badly for everyone involved. He stood from the car and walked to the gates. Slinging them open with a glance, he turned to the guards. "I have no quarrels with any of you. I advise you to leave now lest you be considered my enemy," he shouted. The guards lowered their weapons and allowed Christian to pass through the gates.

He walked up the long drive while Markus followed closely behind in the car. Lucas walked out of the front entrance as Christian arrived. "I see you have not heeded my warning; what shall my recourse be?" Christian demanded.

Lucas hung his head, "Some of the elders feel that it is wrong for you to demand Parliament relocate," he stammered.

"Is that right?" Christian growled, "They refused me leniency, after all of the sacrifices I have made for them, and they feel wronged because I am taking my property back, the very same property they have expelled me from!" Christian became irate. He raised his arm and willed the doors of the front entrance open. They slammed against the exterior walls with his force.

Christian proceeded up the steps stopping next to Lucas. "As a final token of our past friendship, I suggest you leave my estate now," he hissed, as he proceeded through the still-swinging doors.

Christian barged into the chambers and found several of the elders standing about the room. They spun to face him as he entered. "I do not want this evening to end in bloodshed, your only option in preventing it is for you to leave now," he demanded.

William and Frederick approached him. "Our votes were not with the others, we have no quarrel with you," William said as they walked from the room to leave the estate.

Ruth and Isaac stood their ground in front of the podium. Christian slowly raised his head and glared at them. "You will die where you stand if you do not follow them," he warned.

Ruth attempted to have Christian understand their decision, citing their laws on enforcement, but her words only infuriated him further.

"I know the laws, I wrote them!" Christian growled. "You have chosen not to honor my wishes - you have chosen death!" he screamed, as he lunged at her. Moments later both Ruth and Isaac lay in a bloodied heap at the foot of the podium.

Christian turned as he left the room in search of others who chose to remain on his property. Having found no other elders, only security and staff, Christian walked to the front entrance in hopes that Lucas had taken heed to his warning and left. Once at the front doors, he was relieved to see no one other than Markus and the remaining security standing about. His attention was now drawn to the hangar, as he could hear Lucas' jet firing up to leave the estate and return him to his personal home in Italy.

"Now hear this!" Christian announced from the entrance, "I have reclaimed my estate. Those of you who pledge their loyalty to me are welcome to remain; those of you who remain loyal to the Parliament are free to go with no harm befalling you," he finished.

The security guards stood their ground, signaling that they would remain in his employ. "Very well," Christian said, as he turned to go back inside. "Markus," he tolled, as he walked towards the staircase.

"Yes, Lord," Markus responded meekly. "Gather a detail of guards and remove Isaac's and Ruth's remains from the chambers, take them to the cemetery and have them buried respectfully amongst the other elders," he ordered as he approached the corridor to his private suite.

"Yes, Lord," Markus replied as he walked out of sight.

Markus was very concerned for Christian. In all of his years of service he had never witnessed his master in such a vicious light. He had heard stories of his lust for blood led to him having been cursed, and only intensified his viciousness thereafter. Markus had only known Christian to be fair and just; he hoped to see his master return soon to his normal demeanor.

Christian sank into the chair across from his bed, his heart heavy from having to enforce his own words by eliminating Ruth and Isaac. Now the grief caused by his actions had added to the pain of his loss of Adrian. He sat quietly in the chair and looked down at the splintered armrests. He smiled as he knew Adrian had done this as a test of her new strength. He looked across to the bed that they had made love on just as the attack was initiated. There, lying on her pillow, was the ruby and diamond encrusted choker that he had selected for her.

Christian rubbed his brow in an attempt to clear his mind to focus on her. He had to resolve this conflict or the pain within him would madden him into becoming the vicious murderer that he had been after the loss of Cassandra. What would Adrian think of him if he continued to spill blood in her name? "She would not approve," he sighed.

He stood and walked over to the bed, grasped the choker in his hand, and lay down in an attempt to focus on her; perhaps her guard was down and he would be able to communicate with her. Christian closed his eyes and envisioned her face. He could see her briefly. He knew that she was in bed and had the pups with her.

Adrian's eyes flew open as she felt him prying into her mind. She could see the events of the evening as she allowed him to enter. "What have you done, Christian?" she asked, as she saw Ruth and Isaac in their last moments.

She could see he was at the Grenoble estate and sensed he was the only Vampire there. She assumed all of the elders had met their demise in the same fashion. She began to push him out of her mind as she was now terrified by his actions.

This maddened Christian beyond words; he stood from the bed and threw the diamond choker into the nearest wall, where it shattered. The gems glistened in the moonlight as they scattered to the floor. Christian fell to the floor as well and sobbed, as he knew Adrian likely would not leave her guard down again.

Adrian began to pace the cold bedroom floor. She had a decision to make. She knew if she did not go to him his anger would consume and destroy him. He would become a monster and eliminate anyone who reminded him of her. She also knew that if she went to him she would likely surrender her heart to him once more and live in distrust, and perhaps he would take his grief out on her at some point. She lit a cigarette and sat across from the bed, staring blankly at the still-sleeping pups. Her eyes filled with tears at the complexity of her dilemma. She knew that if she called him, he would locate her immediately. She felt she should reach out to him, but knew in her weakened state she would fall back into his arms, which was not an option at this time for her. "I do still love him," she whispered, hoping that he had not heard her. Adrian stood from the chair and crawled back into the bed, curling up around her pups in search of rest.

Several days had passed since Christian had reclaimed his Grenoble property. He had not left his suite. Markus paced the floors of the lower level out of concern for his master. Perhaps he should go to him and convince him to feed tonight. Markus reflected upon Christian's previous threat to him while at the New Orleans estate, and chose a different approach. He trudged down the hallway to meet with Sarah. "I want you to send a donor up to Lord Christian. Go with the donor and see if there is anything he requires," Markus ordered.

Sarah bit her lip but agreed; moments later, she was ushering Christian's donor down the corridor and up the staircase to the entrance of Christian's private suite.

Sarah knocked gently and entered the room to see Christian sitting at a chair in front of the fireplace. His empty eyes stared up at her, irritated with her for having disturbed him.

"Lord, Markus has sent a donor to you. I came along to see what it is I can do for you to make your stay more comfortable," she said softly.

Christian remained seated and silent. He did not utter a word, even as the donor threaded the needle of the IV into his arm. After an uncomfortable silence, he muttered . . . "Find Adrian," as he looked up at Sarah, knowing full well that she was not capable of the task.

"We will do what we can" Sarah replied, as she tidied up the suite.

Christian remained motionless and silent for the remainder of their imposition. Once they left him alone he stood from his seat. Feeling refreshed, he began to organize his thoughts on how he would locate Adrian. In his present situation he did not know who to trust. In order to recruit, he would have to contact the head of each clan, inform them of recent events, and determine where their loyalties would lie. Those that chose to stand by him he would recruit to search for her through whatever means possible; those that opposed him would likely become casualties.

He would begin with William and Frederick, as they had voiced their position to him at last contact.

Christian dialed Frederick's number and arranged for a meeting with them at the Grenoble estate on the following night. Frederick and William both seemed eager to help, as well as eager for changes in the governing policies of the Vampire Nation. Christian would name the brothers as his personal liaisons in recruiting for the new body of government, as well as in the search for Adrian.

Now feeling he had made progress instead of sitting stagnant, Christian would also contact his longtime ally Darian and inform him of the recent turn of events in an attempt to recruit him as one of the elders in his new Parliament. His newfound task had given him purpose and in turn taken his mind off of Adrian, but only for a short while.

.

Chapter Nineteen

Adrian awoke to the puppies playing beside her in the bed. She propped herself upon her elbows to watch them wrestling with each other. "Oh, such fierce children!" she giggled as they took turns pouncing on each other.

She rolled from the bed and began to dress, as she would need to arrange a meeting with the contact Vincent had given her. She retrieved the card from the coat pocket she had worn that night; on the back of the card was scribbled, "Matthew 555-7201".

Adrian sat next to the bed where the puppies were still at play. She lifted her phone and began to dial.

"Hello," a male voice answered.

"Matthew?" she asked.

"Yes, who is this?" he responded.

"Matthew, my name is Adrian, Vincent gave me your contact information. I need to arrange a meeting with you," she explained.

"Ah, yes, Vincent told me to expect a call from you," he said. "I am free this evening," he replied.

"Perfect; where do I meet you?" Adrian asked.

Matthew gave her an address and directions. Soon she was off to start the process of gaining her new identity.

A short while later she was pulling into the drive of the address Matthew had provided to her. The house was a lovely two-story brick home, which sat on the rear of a lot in what appeared to be an upscale suburban development. Adrian parked the car and headed for the front door. Upon ringing the doorbell, a tall figure appeared and opened the door.

"You're Adrian?" the handsome stranger inquired.

"Yes," she answered, as she admired him.

"I'm Matthew," he said, as he ushered her inside, smiling broadly as she walked past him. "So, what is it that I can do to help a beautiful young woman such as yourself?" Matthew flirted.

Adrian smiled at his taunt and responded, "I need a new identity."

Matthew nodded as he motioned for her to enter his office. "Seems we all are running from something." He smiled broadly, exposing his fangs.

Adrian was relieved to know he was Vampire. She found him very attractive, and wondered if Christian had turned him as well. She continued to watch him intently as he turned his back to gather some necessary documents. Adrian admired his ass as he worked.

"So," he said as he turned to her, "We shall fill out these forms, I will need to take a photograph of you and within forty-eight hours you will have your new identity," Matthew smiled as he sat across from her.

She could feel him staring at her as she filled out the paperwork. She decided to confront him as she could read his thoughts. "I find you quite attractive, but I am not looking for a mate," she said as she glanced up at him.

Matthew seemed embarrassed she had read his thoughts.

"I am flattered, though," she added to help him brush off his embarrassment.

Matthew smiled, as he accepted the signed documents from her. "Adrian Fury," he read, "I like it!" he said as he glanced over the papers at her.

"Follow me." he said as he held his hand out to her. "I need a photograph of that lovely face," he said laughing.

Adrian followed him and placed her back against a blue square painted onto the wall. Matthew centered her into the square and went to his camera. "Closed mouth, please," he said, as he pointed at his fangs. Adrian closed her lips just as the photo was snapped.

"That's it," he said as he ushered her back to her seat. "So, what do I owe you for all of this?" she inquired.

"I would love to see you naked," Matthew smiled back at her. "I'm kidding!" he laughed. "Since you were referred to me by Vincent, I will handle all of the arrangements for fifteen thousand. This will include I.D., passport, credit cards and Social Security number," he ended.

Adrian nodded and stood from her seat. "Thank you," she said as she turned for the door. "Call me when they are finished."

"Of course." Matthew said, as he walked her out.

He stood and watched her until she had safely returned to her car and started the engine.

"Nice guy," Adrian whispered to herself as she shifted the car into gear.

Adrian turned onto the highway as she left Matthew's subdivision. She realized that she had not fed for days and decided she would detour through one of the tourist communities in search of prey before returning home.

She decided to walk the back streets as she had before. The area seemed a bit rough to her. "Surely I will happen upon some unsavory character in no time," she thought, as she parked her car.

Adrian walked down the dimly lit, pub lined streets. Several blocks from her car she encountered by a young black male.

"What you doin' in the 'hood, Miss thang? You must be lost," he sneered.

"I am looking for someone," she replied.

"Oh, I can be your someone," he replied, as he grabbed his crotch at her.

Adrian looked at him in disgust as she continued to walk.

"Bitch, you ain't gonna come in to my 'hood and disrespect me!" he yelled behind her.

Adrian continued to walk, giving him the opportunity to live or die.

The thug ran up behind her and grabbed her around her throat. She allowed him to drag her into the alley between two rundown buildings. He slammed her against the wall behind a pile of rubbish.

Adrian stood calmly and smiled at him as he unlatched his belt. "Are you going to rape me?" she asked.

"Yeah, I'm going to rape your fine white ass," he responded as he dropped his pants.

She waited patiently for him to draw near her.

The thug slammed himself into her. As he attempted to penetrate her, she sank her fangs into his neck and began to drain him. She held him close to her as he struggled to free himself. The harder he struggled, the tighter she clutched him to her until his spine snapped. She drained him completely leaving the thug's limp body now crumpled to her feet. Adrian wiped her mouth and walked from the alley to return to her car, having no remorse for her actions.

She smiled as she started the car and headed for home. Upon her arrival, Sheba and Caesar bounded from the small door that she had installed for them; they pranced around the car, waiting for her to exit. "Getting brave, are we?" she laughed, as they ran each other over to greet her. Adrian reached down and scooped the both of them up into her arms. "You know the day will come when you both will not fit into my arms" she said as she kissed their heads. Adrian carried them back inside and decided to shower off the traces of the young thug that she had fed upon before changing into more comfortable clothes.

Now changed, she made her way to the study in order to select and research her next fugitive. As she signed on to the Most-Wanted website, she saw a newsflash appear; a picture of Brown slid across the screen with "CAPTURED" stamped in red over his face. She felt a sense of accomplishment as she stared at his photo. "One down," she muttered as she began to search through the other fugitive photos.

She found that the same three that stood out to her before were calling to her once more. She chose the third of the three, Elias Moorefield.

She began to compile information on Moorefield, realizing he would be much more dangerous than Brown. His arrest record was extensive; he was known to be armed and dangerous. She would have to devise a new strategy in order to successfully obtain him. All of her data, as well as her instincts, indicated that he was in New Orleans; she was reluctant to return there, but relieved because she knew the area well.

She closed her file and turned to see the pups still wrestling on the floor behind her. "Come to me," she said as she held her arms out to them. She lifted them into her lap and lavished them with affection.

"Are you hungry?" she asked, as she carried them into the kitchen for their evening feeding. The pups ate well and were soon ready to retire for the day, and Adrian was as well. "Go outside," she told them before sleep could overtake them.

She giggled as they groggily staggered through the pet door for their evening outing. She sat on the edge of the couch and waited patiently for their return, Sheba was first through the door, and Caesar followed slowly behind her. They sat at her feet and looked up at her yawning. Adrian smiled as she scooped them up and carried them to her suite.

They, now familiar with the routine, found their spot at the foot of the bed and curled up onto each other. Soon they were sound asleep. Adrian flipped the lever that lowered all of the steel shutters around her home and returned to the bed. As had been her routine as of late, she began to focus on Christian out of concern. She could see him talking with an older man; it was an intense conversation. She now knew he was not alone and was content to sleep through the day.

She arose early the next day, several hours before sunset. The pups still slept soundly at the foot of the bed. She decided to go upstairs and continue her research on Moorefield. She would have another day to wait until her new identification was ready, so in using her time wisely she would know all that there was to know about her newest target.

Nearly an hour had passed. She was so absorbed in her studies that she did not notice the pups had made their way upstairs and were patiently waiting at her feet for breakfast. Sheba barked, startling her. "When did you learn to do that?" she laughed, as she turned to see the pups staring back at her. She leaned over and began to rub their heads. "Have we been outside yet?" she asked. The pups ran for their door and Adrian stood to put food in their bowl for their return.

She began to think about her trip to New Orleans and wondered if Christian would know if she was there. Her house had not sold yet, so she could stay there if necessary, but was it worth the risk, she thought. "I will decide tomorrow" she said aloud, as she returned to her computer to finish her research.

Christian had spent another sleepless night in meetings with some of the other elders. Most of them supported him in his efforts to create a new, more modern-minded Parliament. By the end of the past evening he had named two more elders to hold seats and had assigned them to modernize the laws that he had written with Lucas and Isaac so many centuries past.

Though the changes he had demanded were now taking form, he was still empty inside, with the exception of the venom, which had built within him over the loss of Adrian. Nothing seemed to quell his thirst for vengeance, and he had become more desperate to find her.

Suddenly, he came to the realization Adrian would not have left the United States; though she had been grief-stricken to the point of leaving her home, she would not have left her country. He summoned William and Frederick and informed them that he would be returning to his New Orleans estate that evening. He instructed them on the tasks he would want them to have completed upon his return. He then called for Markus and instructed for him to have the jet prepared to leave for New Orleans at sundown.

Christian retreated to his suite in order to rest before his flight. As he climbed the stairs, his thoughts turned to Lucas. Perhaps he should reach out once more to him before leaving the country.

Christian sat next to the phone and considered what he might say to Lucas. In frustration, he snatched the phone and began to dial the number for Lucas' estate in Italy. A young female answered.

"I must speak with Lucas, please," he replied to her greeting. He patiently waited for Lucas to pick up the line.

"Yes?" he answered.

"Lucas, it's Christian, I wanted to try to speak with you once more before returning to the States," he said.

"Christian, it seems we have nothing further to discuss. We disagree on what the standards of our laws should be, and now you have bloodied your hands to make the changes you see fit," Lucas replied.

Christian sighed heavily as he could see Lucas refused to change his position. "I value our friendship, but things do change. We cannot run our nation off of laws that are antiquated. Our laws must change throughout time lest we stagnate and die off," Christian pleaded.

"I am sorry, but I will not change my mind," Lucas stated adamantly. A moment of silence passed between the two of them before Christian spoke once more, "I wish you well old friend," he said solemnly as he hung up the phone.

Saddened that he could not sway Lucas from his old way of thinking in one sense, but gratified he had made the effort to reach out to him one last time. Christian collapsed across the bed with a clear conscience and rested for the remainder of the day.

Chapter Twenty

Adrian had worked fiercely at her research through the day and into the evening. She decided that she had had enough and would spend some time with the pups, since she would be gone for the next couple of days.

She sat in the floor and tussled with them, playing with them until they were exhausted and had curled up into her lap to sleep. "Aren't we the lively bunch?" she chuckled, as she stood with them in her arms. As she made her way into the den, her phone rang. She had only given the number to two people so far, the contractor and Matthew. Assuming that it was Matthew, she rushed to answer.

"Hello?" she answered.

"Ms. Adrian Fury, I have your paperwork ready," Matthew said.

"Awesome!" she replied. "I will be there shortly to pick it up," she responded.

"I am looking forward to seeing you." Matthew answered seductively.

Adrian smirked at his advance, but found it amusing. She hung up the phone and changed clothes before leaving. "Stay inside," she ordered the pups as she left.

A while later, she was pulling up to Matthew's house, cash in hand. He met her at the door in a pair of tight jeans with no shirt. She had to admit he was quite attractive to her.

He ushered her through the door and into his office. "You look gorgeous this evening." he said as he ogled her.

Adrian sat back into her chair and grinned at him. "Matthew, you are very good-looking. If things in my life were different right now, I would certainly take advantage of you; but the timing is not right for me," she said as she scanned his muscular chest with her eyes.

"Hopefully things will change," he said as he sat on the desk across from her, his crotch displayed directly in her line of sight. She smiled and shook her head at his attempt. "Let's see what you have created for me," she blurted out, in order to avoid staring between his legs.

Matthew stretched across the desk, retrieved a box and handed it to her. Adrian opened the box and examined the documents.

"These are perfect!" she said, smiling broadly. She reached into her back pocket and retrieved the envelope that contained his payment. Matthew opened the envelope and peered down into it. "Are you sure that you won't reconsider my previous offer?" he smiled. Adrian stood and approached him where he still sat on the edge of his desk. "I will take a rain check," she said, as she brushed her soft lips across his cheek.

He shivered as she kissed him. "You are a tease," he said smiling.

"Thanks again Matthew," she said as she walked out of the house, waving the box of documents at him.

"Bye gorgeous!" he called behind her as she climbed into her car.

Adrian laughed at Matthew the entire way home. His advances had given her a reason to feel good about herself. Though she had no intention of following through, it was good to know that she was desirable.

She wheeled into the garage and entered through the side door to find Sheba and Caesar waiting by the door for her where she had left them. She realized at that moment she would not be able to leave them alone again. "You little shits," she laughed, "I suppose I will have to fly first class with you two from now on," she laughed as she leaned down to pet them.

She walked directly to her desk and booked a first-class flight for two seats to New Orleans for early the next evening. She turned to watch the puppies at play just as Sheba had pounced on Caesar. "Oh, the fierceness of it all!" she laughed as they tumbled over one another. Now with the puppies would be traveling with her, she had decided to stay at her home just outside of New Orleans.

She had to prepare herself for Christian appearing while she was there. Adrian sank into the couch. Had she subconsciously set herself up for this? Was this why she had been drawn to this particular fugitive? She sat numbly and tried to sort through her thoughts and feelings.

The bounty hunter tangent she had been on had distracted her from thinking about Christian, but now she was forced to prepare herself for a possible encounter with him. "I have to face this." she said aloud.

She stood and paced the floors as she cited the pros and cons of her situation. "I love him, but now I cannot trust him. He is hurting and he needs me, but he turned his back on me when I needed him. Why did he do that? He did not leave my side after my mortal death, maybe I owe him the opportunity to explain; but now how will I know if what he is saying is true? Maybe I will call him to me when I get to my house. That way, if things aren't right, I can still come back here, out of his sight," she pondered.

She continued to pace, trying to separate the emotional from the logical, to no avail. She collapsed back down into the couch, exhausted. Above all of the conflict, she realized that she wanted nothing more than to be in his arms at that moment.

It had been months since the night she fled the Grenoble estate. She had not allowed herself to think back on the event since that night.

Adrian wept from the depths of her soul. She was not aware in the outpouring of her pent-up emotions, her defenses had been weakened. Christian heard her wailing.

The sound of her sobs melted him; his heart felt as though it would burst. He slumped to his knees; now emotional, he could not summon the power to locate her. He was furious as he was helpless to find her, unable to hold her and comfort her. His venom boiled over. He vowed death to everyone involved in making her suffer.

The pilot announced their final descent. Markus walked into the cabin to check on Christian before they landed. He found his Lord crumpled to the floor sobbing. Markus decided to return to the cockpit, as Christian had not noticed him enter. He hung his head as he closed the door silently behind him.

Markus' thoughts returned to Christian's bloody past when he had lost Cassandra. For decades Christian had roamed the countryside in search of everyone responsible for her death, as well as anyone known to be friend or family. Markus prayed that his Master was not returning to that state, as he had vowed his loyalty to Christian for the remainder of his life.

The plane soon skidded to a stop at the New Orleans estate. Christian rose from the floor and washed his face.

He was completely drained as he made his way down the steps and to the back of the hangar, as it was now daylight and he would have to enter through the underground corridor.

Markus met up with Christian as he entered the main floor. "Allow me to send up a donor, Lord," he whispered in Christian's ear. Christian nodded and patted Markus on his back as he proceeded to his suite.

As soon as Christian settled in his bed, Markus was ushering two donors to his bedside. Christian closed his eyes as the donors inserted their IV's into him. "Thank you, Markus," he said, as he surrendered to sleep.

Adrian had slept soundly as exhaustion had taken her over earlier that day. She had several hours to prepare for her flight. She packed her bag and found a separate bag for the pups. She called ahead and rented a car and soon was ready to leave. "Come" she called to the pups as she lowered their bag to the ground. The pups clambered into the bag and sat obediently as she lifted them and carried them to the car. She was on her way now, back to what she once knew as home.

The drive was somber as she planned the stages of her mission. Soon she was boarding the plane bound for New Orleans. Adrian sat the pups on the aisle seat as she seated herself next to the window. Within moments she was watching the skyline as they soared over Memphis.

Suddenly, she was surprised by the appearance of a flight attendant. "Can I get you a drink?" she smiled.

"Crown and Coke" Adrian requested.

"Oh, look at these little guys!" the attendant cooed as she reached to pet Sheba and Caesar. Sheba snapped immediately as Caesar managed a fierce growl.

Adrian chuckled at them. "I'm sorry, they're a little antisocial," she explained, as the startled girl snatched her hand away. The attendant poured her drink and carefully handed it to her. "Thanks," Adrian said, as she turned to look back out at the starlit sky. She would be back at her former home within the next three hours. Adrian began to feel anxious, thinking of what may await her before the evening was finished.

Christian rested well and awoke refreshed. He sat up on the corner of his bed and determined that he would start his search for her at her home just outside of the city. He knew full well that she would not be there, but hoped that he would be able to gather some sense of where she might be. He stood and ran his fingers through his tousled hair, then turned to see her shoe sitting where he had left it on the chair near the fireplace. He sighed as he thought back to the pain he had felt from her only hours ago.

Christian staggered into the shower. The hot water woke his senses as he leaned against the wall and let it flow over his taut body. He fought the urge to let his emotions take over him as he focused intently on her. With no sense of where she was or what she was doing, he climbed from the shower and began dressing to head downstairs.

Christian proceeded to the main level of the house and was immediately summoned to the phone. "Christian, its Frederick. I thought you would want to know Lucas has been here demanding the recordings of the Parliament for the duration of his holding the chair," he said.

"And what came of it?" Christian asked.

"We declined him entrance to the estate, as well as the journals," Frederick replied.

"Stay alert as he will not have taken your denial lightly. Put security on twelve-hour shifts and add more manpower, I suspect this will not be the only visit that you will receive in my absence," he finished.

"Yes, Lord," Frederick answered.

Christian hung the phone up and began to question why Lucas would have interest in the journals. There was no one for him to plead a case to, as he had made contact with all remaining elders and sensed that none of them would oppose him.

Christian thought for a moment more and then called Frederick back.

"Yes, Lord," Frederick answered.

"I want you and William to contact all of the other elders and record their locations, and find out which of them have been in contact with Lucas by any means necessary," he ordered. "Report your findings back to me as soon as you have results" he finished.

"Yes, Lord" Frederick replied again as he ended the call to pursue his tasks.

Christian lifted the phone once more and called Markus to bring the car around. Within minutes he had climbed into the back seat and they were on their way.

Adrian had made her way to the rental car desk and was signing the last of the forms. She lugged at her bags as she spotted the car, the last Cadillac on the lot and of course in the most remote parking space available. Finally, she threw her luggage into the back seat and placed the curious pups in the passenger seat beside her. She pulled away from the parking lot and fought her way into Interstate traffic. Soon she would be crossing the Bonnet Carré Spillway and on her way home.

It felt odd to her to be back in the area, as she had set her old life so far behind her in the past months. She smiled at the familiar bayous that lined the elevated Interstate north of the city. An hour later she was pulling up to the gate of her former home. It appeared abandoned and lonely to her.

She drove to the garage and parked her car inside. She had noticed her cell phone was no longer sitting in front of the door where she had left it. She assumed the Realtor had picked it up when showing the house.

Adrian walked through the door and flipped the light on. She stood and stared into her lonely home; there were so many sad memories now attached to this place that she had once so loved. She sighed as she sat the puppies on the floor, motioning for them to crawl out of the bag, then led them to the laundry room and directed them to the pet door.

Though there was a woeful air about her, the house looked good; very different from her previous décor, as she had hired an interior decorator to stage the interior for marketing purposes. The property was a high-ticket item for the area it was in. Adrian knew it would not sell quickly and counted on having it to come to for several months if necessary.

She sat her keys down on the bar and began to admire the décor. Now that it was winter, she thought perhaps she should check and make sure that the pool was being maintained.

Adrian walked towards the rear of the house, pausing where her friend and pet had lost their lives. Her heart grew heavy as she stared at the clean floor and fresh paint, which revealed no sign of the past. Slowly she moved forward and entered the master suite and then to the patio, where she flipped the light switch to see the sparkling water of the pool glistening back at her. Adrian truly had loved her home and considered that maybe she had made a rash decision in putting it on the market. She stood and stared at her grounds with mixed emotions. Saddened, she turned to go back inside the house.

Markus had pulled the car up the Adrian's gate and entered the code. Christian eagerly looked about the grounds and saw the Realtor's "For Sale" sign. He hung his head as the sign made an overwhelming statement to him. He noticed that as they approached the house most of the lights were on, but assumed that it was for security purposes since the house was now vacant.

Markus stopped at the end of the circle drive and remained in the car as Christian walked to the front door to find that it was unlocked. Cautiously, he entered the house not knowing what or who to expect. Finding Adrian there was the furthest from his mind at that moment. Christian quietly closed the door behind him and proceeded through the den to see if anything had been disturbed. As he entered the hallway he looked up to see Adrian walking from the master suite. The two of them froze in their tracks.

Chapter Twenty-One

Adrian melted as her eyes fell into his, half of her wanting to run to him, the other half wanting to run away. As she fought within herself, her body flooded with adrenaline; she was primed to run, yet she stood frozen in place. "How did I not sense he was here?" she thought.

At that moment she realized that she was out of time to prepare herself for the eminent encounter. Christian took a step towards her and then fell to his knees. His eyes begged her for mercy as he looked up into her face and pleaded, "Please forgive me, please let me explain."

Adrian's eyes began fill with tears, she fought them back, managing only to say, "You turned your back on me. You broke my heart."

"Please forgive me, you don't understand," he pleaded, as he stumbled to his feet and placed his hand upon her cheek.

"I don't understand, how can I?" she answered as she began to sob.

Christian pulled her to him and held her; nothing else seemed to matter at the moment. Slowly she began to accept and return his embrace. They fell to their knees together in the hallway. Together they released all of their emotions. Without a word said they sat and wept, for their pain, for their love and for their loss.

Christian was the first to break the silence as he began to explain his side of the situation to her. "I did not have time to discuss things with you. There is a process," he began. "Had I looked into your eyes at the time before the trial, we would have considered as having calculated this series of cursed events. The Parliament could have been much harsher in their judgment." Christian realized it all sounded so inane, he hung his head as he uttered, "None of this matters now."

She assumed he meant it did not matter because she was in his arms once more, though she was still conflicted over if she belonged there.

Christian continued to explain. "I have disassembled the Parliament and evicted them from the estate. Our sentencing is now irrelevant," he said smugly.

She grew flustered at his words, "Fuck Parliament! How could you have sat and allowed them to do what they did to me? This is not about the elders, this is about you and me!" she said weakly, as her tears had drained her.

"You must understand I formed the Parliament and, with you as my chosen mate, we were most obligated to abide by its rules" he explained. "We represent the entire Vampire Nation," he finished.

"As far as I am concerned, the entire Vampire Nation as I know it, to include my mate, turned its back on me for doing nothing more than fighting to protect it!" she moaned.

"I know your pain, as I have grieved with you. I have destroyed what I had built in order to reform a new nation, as the old way had dishonored you," he stated with a bit of a scowl in his voice. "Blood has been shed in your name. I have eliminated all that could ever threaten our happiness again," he said, as he held her away in order to look her in her beautiful yet tormented blue eyes.

"What more can I do to earn your trust? Name it and it shall be yours," he said, searching her eyes for some hint of forgiveness.

She bowed her head and placed it on his shoulder. Though she was still filled with pain, she could stand to see him suffer any more. She drew her hands to his head and pulled him near to her; they stood in an embrace and wept once more. "I never stopped loving you, Christian," she whispered, "but this has devastated me and now I am different from how you once knew me," she finished.

He held her even tighter than ever before. "No one will ever come between us again without knowing more pain than the two of us combined have suffered through," he whispered back to her.

Christian was distracted by a strange noise behind him; he turned to see Caesar and Sheba ready to pounce with their hair on edge. They were none too happy with him being anywhere near Adrian.

"Oh, my fierce ones!" Adrian sighed, "Come to me," she said as she leaned over to pick them up and introduce them to Christian. "Children, this is Christian," she said, as she lifted them from the floor. "This is Sheba and Caesar," she said as she motioned to each one separately.

"They are truly handsome," Christian replied with a smile.

Adrian proceeded to tell him the story of how she came to have the pups.

Christian reached over to pet the pups. Caesar did not seem to mind however, Sheba was not as accepting of him. Adrian kissed the pups on their heads and sat them back down on the floor. As she stood, Christian held out his arm to her and ushered her to the patio to sit on the lounge chair. "Stay here," he said, as she settled. "I'll be right back," he shouted over his shoulder as he rushed away.

A few moments later he had returned from his car with two glasses and a bottle of wine for them. He sat next to her and poured the pungent Merlot into the crystal glasses. "Do you remember the first time that we sat here together?" he asked.

Adrian smiled as she thought back to the beginning of their relationship, truly happier days. She remembered this was the same place that he had told her he was in love with her. It felt like a lifetime had passed since they were happy together.

"We will both have to work very hard to repair the damage done," she said as she watched the puppies playing on the lawn.

Christian handed her a glass of wine and turned to face her. "I am more than willing to do whatever it takes," he smiled warmly.

"Please be patient with me," she sighed. "It will be more difficult for me as I am also battling with the changes within me," she finished.

"Understood," he said, as he leaned forward and placed a soft kiss on her forehead. "So, if I may ask, what brought you back here this evening?" he inquired.

She smiled as she answered, "A fugitive."

His expression changed to one of confusion. Before he could ask, she decided to elaborate.

"I decided to try my hand at bounty hunting. I turned in my first fugitive last week, and have tracked my second to New Orleans," she said.

Christian's forehead wrinkled in concern. "I would think that to be a bit dangerous."

Adrian smirked at his response, "Let's just say I have begun to understand some of my abilities, and furthermore with the state of mind that I have been in recently, I am not the one that has been in danger," she added confidently.

"I suppose not," he chuckled. "Have you fed recently?" he asked.

"Yes, before I came here," she said as she sipped at her wine.

"So you are no longer having difficulty with that, then?"

"I go through extremes to find the right prey," she uttered as she looked into the starlit sky.

"I see," he nodded. "It does get easier in time to be less selective about who you feed upon" he said as he lit a cigarette for her.

"Perhaps," she replied as she chose her next words carefully. "Though I am no longer human, I choose not to forget the value of a human life," she finished.

Christian smiled and nodded, realizing she had not completely left her mortal ways behind as of yet. "I do not want you to take this the wrong way, but you do need to understand you are a superior being. You are superior amongst superior beings, and you are my mate," he said carefully.

Adrian sat quietly as she absorbed his words; though she knew there was truth in them, she was uncomfortable with the notion.

"I am at a bit of an overload right now," she finally responded. She stood and began to pace. "My entire world has been turned completely upside down and shaken violently within the past few months. I am afraid both mentally and emotionally I do not have the capacity to handle that way of thinking along with rebuilding our relationship while learning how to be a Vampire!" she blurted out on the verge of tears once more. "This is all just too fucking much!" she muttered as she turned her back to him.

Christian walked over to her and wrapped his arms around her from behind while placing his head on her shoulder. "I understand, I will be here beside you and we will get through all of this together," he whispered.

She found comfort in his words as she knew he was committed to her, though she knew she would have great difficulty overcoming her own doubts. "Dawn is approaching. Shall we continue this discussion inside?" he asked gingerly.

Adrian nodded and called for the pups as they walked into the house, lowering the shutters behind them.

Christian and Adrian spent the next few hours in deep conversation in an attempt to heal their tattered relationship. By sunset the following day, he had convinced her to join him at his New Orleans estate, where the staff would be there to serve her.

Their reunion at the New Orleans estate remained casual, as Adrian still found herself hesitant to fall immediately back into their relationship. Christian was happy just to have her back within eyesight, as he knew that she would need time to adjust on many levels.

The following evening came with the announcement Adrian would be leaving the estate in search of Moorefield. Christian was extremely unsettled with the idea of her leaving his sight but knew that if he objected he might push her away. Grudgingly, he agreed, as he watched her place the files into her briefcase.

"It's not that I don't think you are more than capable of apprehending this Moorefield, I am just worried you are putting yourself at risk," he implored one last time.

Adrian was becoming irritated with him. "This is something I feel drawn to do Christian. Maybe it is my human mentality calling me to do this, but until I am no longer subject to those feelings, I ask you honor my intentions," she said calmly.

Christian ran his fingers through his hair and chuckled. "Stubbornness apparently will never be an attribute that weakens within you," he said as he sat across the room from her and stared at her shoe that he had placed in the chair opposite of him days ago. He could only smile as he thought how heartsick he was when he had first discovered it, and now she had returned to him.

Though she was there with him now, she was very different. He found her to be empty and distracted. Christian grew concerned, as she was a new Vampire who possessed abilities that no other ever had, and she had been subjected to so much in the past few months. "I will honor your wishes; you are free to do as you please," he sighed.

Christian realized that he was not only worried for Adrian's safety; he was deeply concerned that she would have difficulty learning to bridle the force within her. No Vampire had ever fed from more than two elders so soon upon being turned, or within such a brief span of time.

Adrian lifted her briefcase and walked across the room. She stopped at the door and turned to him. "Thank you. Your support does mean a lot to me," she said dryly as she turned to leave for the evening.

Christian rubbed his chin as he watched her walk through the door and into the hallway. For one brief moment he considered following her while she completed her mission. His better judgment would call for him to give her the distance, which she had requested.

She walked from the main entrance to see Markus standing next to the limo. "May I take you somewhere this evening Ms. Adrian?" he asked.

"No thanks Markus, I'll be driving myself" she replied as she walked to her car and started the engine. She drove through the front gate, opened the file on Moorefield and placed a photo of him in her lap as she proceeded. "Where are you tonight, Moorefield?" she asked. Moments later, visions of his surroundings began to flash before her eyes. She could see him outside of a dingy nightclub. He wasn't alone. "This may be more complicated than I had expected" she mumbled to herself. "No matter, I am up to the challenge," she smiled.

Chapter Twenty-Two

Adrian drove by instinct through the back streets of New Orleans, thankful that she did not have to be intimidated by her surroundings; she was more than capable of defending herself. Soon she felt that she had found her destination.

She pulled into a parking lot; she knew that she was definitely in gang territory. There on the corner was an old cinderblock building surrounded by thugs. As she scanned the crowd outside, Moorefield stood out to her. It was as if she were looking at him through an infrared scope. She remained in the car and observed him and the group around him, realizing that they were there to protect him.

Adrian watched as the group moved towards a car in the far side of the parking lot where she sat. She knew they were not preparing to leave as she watched while they passed a blunt amongst themselves. "Perfect," she mumbled aloud.

She crept from the car and floated above them. There were nine in all, counting Moorefield. Adrian landed directly in front of Moorefield, looked into his eyes and said, "You will not move from this spot!" as she drew two daggers from her waistline. Two of the group fled as she turned to face them, baring her fangs and hissing; the remainder of the group frantically armed themselves.

She strategically placed herself between them and Moorefield, who stood frozen and terrified. Adrian began to fight with the surrounding thugs, first eliminating their firearms so as not to draw the attention of gunfire. Wildly she slashed at them. Within seconds, all but one were lying dead at her feet.

The one remaining thug was badly injured and dragging his left leg behind him as he struggled to run away. She jumped into the air and landed in front of him.

Adrian bared her fangs at him as he fell to the ground and begged for his life. She lifted him by his hair and bit into his neck. He screamed until she tore away his throat, then fed upon him until she had bled him dry. With nothing more to satisfy her, she released his head and his carcass fell to the ground before Moorefield.

Adrian slowly turned and stared into Moorefield's eyes, who, in turn urinated on himself.

"Filthy fucking thug," she said as she slowly approached him. "Walk" she ordered as she peered into his fear-stricken eyes. "Not such a vicious bastard now, are you?" she taunted him.

Adrian shoved him in the direction of her parked car and opened the trunk. "Get in and shut up" she said. Moorefield obediently climbed into the trunk and curled into a fetal position as he trembled uncontrollably. She climbed into the car and called the U. S. Marshall's office, advising them that she was bringing Moorefield in and expected the reward to be waiting for her upon her arrival.

Within a few minutes she pulled up to the front of the office. Several deputies stood awaiting her.

"Good evening boys," she said as she stood from the car. "Who is in charge here?" she asked.

A tall man began to approach her. "I am Captain Freleaux," he said as he held his hand out to her.

"Good to meet you" she said as she shook his hand. Adrian walked around to the rear of the car and popped the trunk to display Moorefield still lying in a fetal position.

"Get out of there and go with this man," she ordered.

Moorefield climbed from the trunk and stood in front of her. Adrian passed her hand in front of his face and mentally erased the happenings of the last hour from his memory.

"Come on boy!" Freleaux ordered, as he grabbed Moorefield by the arm and led him into the complex. Adrian followed behind them and placed a mental command in his head: "Have the deputies start the booking process, then go write my check" she ordered.

Freleaux called for the deputies and directed them to take Moorefield into booking.

"Come with me," he said as he turned to her.

Adrian followed Freleaux into his office and placed her new identification card in front of him. "Make the check out to cash," she said as she looked into his eyes.

Freleaux nodded and pulled a large check register from his top drawer. In no time, she was pocketing her reward and on her way out of the building to her car.

As she drove in the direction of Christian's estate a feeling of empowerment and accomplishment came over her. After having confronted a gang and a known fugitive with no problems, she now knew that she could complete any mission that she saw fit; Adrian became driven to research her next fugitive.

Upon her return to the estate, Adrian saw two male Vampires being escorted from the grand entrance to their waiting limo. She was overcome by a feeling of dread as she watched them. The expression on Christian's face only fueled her suspicions as he stood leaning against the front entrance.

Adrian was eager for an explanation as she stood from her car and approached the entryway. "Who was that?" she asked as the car pulled away toward the gate.

Christian hung his head and sighed, "Nothing for you to worry about, just more political bullshit. How did your bounty hunting go?" he asked in an attempt to change the subject.

She smiled and held up the check, "Quite well," she replied as she took his arm and entered into the foyer.

"Very good," he smiled as he patted her hand. "Come and tell me all about it," he said as he led her to the parlor.

Adrian was distracted by his interest in her new hobby and had forgotten all about the two men that had left such an ill feeling within her. As she spent the next hour describing the events of her evening, she began to feel the closeness between herself and Christian being rejuvenated. They spent the remainder of the dark hours walking hand-in-hand around the lovely estate grounds while sharing a bottle of wine. Adrian's heart was light as she was beginning to feel some semblance of comfort with his presence once more.

She watched Christian in the moonlight as he played with the pups, who had been following them about the grounds. She began to feel flushed with desire for him once more as he tussled with them. Soon after, they were hand-in-hand once more as they approached the grand entrance.

As they entered the front doors, she could fight the urge no longer. She placed her hand on Christian's face and drew him to her. She looked deeply into his eyes, before kissing him softly.

His eyes closed as she touched him. He had feared she may never warm back up to him after the trauma their relationship had been subjected to.

Adrian began to draw away from him; he wrapped his arms around her and pulled her tightly to him. She laid her head upon his broad chest and absorbed his embrace as he stroked her long blonde hair. She could feel the relief of her acceptance pulsing through his body.

Christian sighed as he released her and kissed her lightly on her forehead. "Never doubt my love for you Adrian," he smiled. "I will still require your patience with me," she sighed. "Deep within me, part of me still loves you too, Christian." She smiled back at him as she brushed her hand across his cheek.

He held his arm out to her as he turned to release the steel shutters for the approaching day. "Shall I escort you to your room?" he asked, as the shutters slammed down behind them. "Yes, it has been a long evening," she said, as she walked with him up the staircase.

Christian stopped in front the suite where Adrian had been sleeping since her return and opened the door for her. The pups barged through the door first and leapt into her bed.

"I believe they have some sense of entitlement," she laughed, as they looked on.

"Get some rest," he smiled as he kissed her on her cheek and turned to leave.

Adrian walked into the room and sat next to the pups on her bed. She realized that she was now uncomfortable in knowing that Christian would sleep alone. She could hear him entering his suite next to hers, and knew that he was saddened still by her absence.

Adrian stroked the pups until they fell asleep. She was conflicted with the fact she would be no more uncomfortable sleeping alone than in his presence. Determining that her plight was futile she decided to act spontaneously by surprising Christian. She stood, removed her clothes and made her way out of her room.

Quietly, she opened his door to see him sitting at the fireplace with his back to her. She moved stealthily as she approached, startling him as she appeared before him.

Before he could speak she curled herself into his lap and wrapped her arms around his neck. Christian was surprised indeed. He smiled as he pulled her close to him. He was contented just to hold her and stroke her soft skin.

At that moment they both knew they could be happy again. Christian continued to hold her for quite some time. After a while she realized that her face was wet. She raised her head to see that tears had streaked his beautiful face. She lifted her hands and wiped them away, then kissed him softly on his lips.

"Never again," she whispered in his ear.

He nodded as he pulled her back to him. "I still have felt as though I had lost you, even though you were here with me," he said.

"I am lost myself and have been for quite some time," she responded. Suddenly, they were distracted by the sound of pawing at the door. They smiled at each other as she raised her hand and willed the door open for the pups, then closed it behind them.

"Adapting well to your abilities I see." He smiled as the pups clamored to climb into their laps.

"I'm still learning," she said as she reached down to pet them. Christian raised his hand and pointed at the rug in front of the fireplace. "Go lay down" he said to the pups - to no avail; the pups still stood clamoring to get into the chair.

Adrian giggled at their stubbornness. She looked down at them and said, "Children, go lay by the fireplace."

The pups grudgingly walked to the rug and soon were nestled in for a long sleep.

"Oh, I see," laughed Christian.

Adrian shifted in his lap to face him. "I will enjoy falling in love with you again," she said, as she ran her fingers through his hair.

Christian sighed at her touch and raised her hand up to his face. "I have missed your touch" he whispered.

She leaned forward and placed a soft kiss onto his lush lips. He sighed as she withdrew from him to look into his eyes. "Take me to bed," she told him within her thoughts.

Without breaking eye contact, Christian cradled her in his arms and stood to carry her to his bed. Gently, he laid her onto his bed; still looking into her eyes as he carefully raised his body in position to hover over her. She, with her arms still wrapped around his neck, pulled him to her and kissed him passionately.

Christian's hands began to roam her soft skin. As he reacquainted himself with her body, she could feel him becoming aroused. She slid her hands beneath his shirt and gently removed it from him so that she could once again feel his broad chest against her bare skin.

Christian buried his face into her shoulder as he relished the contact of their bodies together once more. She stroked his back as she kissed his shoulder and wrapped her legs around him in further embrace. Adrian then slid her hands beneath him and unfastened his belt. Slowly, she began to remove his pants with her feet as she grasped his firm ass in her hands.

Nearly breathless at this point, Christian gently began to manipulate his hips in order to find his way into her; she spread her legs widely to greet him. Adrian gasped as he plunged himself into her; it felt as if ages had passed since they had made love. Slowly, he forced himself deeper into her, their eyes locked in passion.

She held her arms up to him, wrapping them around his neck and pulling him towards her. She softly kissed at his neck and shoulders as her hands caressed his strong back. Gently, she lifted her legs and wrapped them around him as she slowly aligned her hips to meet with his upon each stroke.

His eyes bore nothing but love and submissiveness to her; she ran her fingertips down his fangs before placing a deep and passionate kiss upon his mouth. His eyes closed in ecstasy at her touch. She knew that he had longed for her while they had been apart. Adrian began to feel that the pain would pass and she could once again fall fully in love with him.

She wrapped her arms around him tightly and flipped them over. Now on top of him she began to slowly raise and lower herself onto him so that she could feel him in his entirety as she plunged him deeper inside of her with each stroke.

Christian reached up and placed his hands on either side of her face, stroking her cheeks. Adrian reached up and intertwined her fingers with his, holding his hands to her face. She leaned over him and continued to slowly make love to him. She placed a soft kiss on his forehead, then another on his lips as she made her way to his neck. Gently, she sank her fangs into him and began to suck lightly at his warm sweet blood. Christian pulled her closer to him and began to manipulate her hips with his hands, bringing them both to orgasm as she drank from him.

Their orgasm now dwindling, he pulled her down tightly on top of him and held her in his arms. Adrian nestled her head upon his chest and wrapped her arms around him in embrace, where they remained until they had both fallen deeply asleep.

Hours later, she was awakened by Christian moaning and calling out for her. She whispered into his ear, "I am here, my love, here by your side."

The sound of her voice woke him with a jolt. He sat upright in the bed and strained to clear his eyes to see she was truly there beside him. Christian reached out to her and held her tightly.

"I was dreaming I was surrounded by darkness and I had lost you again," he sighed heavily.

Adrian reassuringly stroked at his hair. "You have not lost me, lie back down and hold me," she coaxed.

Christian slid back down next to her in the bed, wrapping himself tightly around her and she around him. They would spend the rest of the day in undisturbed slumber.

Shortly before sunset they were awakened by the pups as they clamored to get into the bed. Christian rolled over and lifted them into the bed with them, both of them competing to be in Adrian's lap.

"Good morning children," she laughed as she held them close to her. Christian looked on, amused by the sight.

"I suppose they're telling you that they need to go outside," he said, as he rolled over to light cigarettes for the both of them.

Adrian willed the door to the suite open and sent the pups outside as she accepted the cigarette from Christian.

"What shall we do this evening?" he asked as he stroked her naked thigh. Adrian thought for a moment, then answered, "I would like to begin research on my next fugitive at some point, but I do have other things in mind for us before that" she smiled, as she leaned over and placed a kiss on his taut stomach.

No sooner had her lips left his skin than the bedside phone rang. Christian smirked as he leaned over to answer. "Yes" he said, followed by a long period of silence.

Adrian began to feel a knot forming in her stomach; whatever was being said on the other end of the call was not good.

Christian sat upright and turned his back to her as he listened intently. He stood abruptly and began to pace the room. By now she had determined that he was talking with William and Frederick. Though she was concerned with the conversation, she could not help but admire his naked profile as he stood in front of the fireplace.

"I will be down in a few minutes," he growled as he ended the call. She determined it best not to ask about the call, but as he turned, it became obvious to her that he was avoiding eye contact with her. "What is it?" she finally blurted out as she watched him sort through his closet. Moments later he exited, throwing a suit onto the foot of the bed as he stormed toward the shower.

Adrian approached him and placed her hands onto his chest, "What is it?" she asked again as she looked into his deep brown eyes.

Christian sighed; he knew he would have to explain the call to her. "It seems that the remaining members of the old Parliament have elected new members and are now meeting to discuss options of overthrowing me and my new Parliament," he surrendered.

Adrian knew because he had slaughtered Ruth and Isaac, they would be eager to seek revenge upon Christian. She hung her head as the thought crossed her mind. Slowly, she walked to the vanity and sat down to ponder her thoughts.

What could she do to stop this? What options did she have in protecting Christian, and the estate? Christian watched as she faded deep into thought; concerned it may have been too much for her to handle, he approached her and wrapped his arms around her.

"This is not for you to concern yourself with," he whispered as he pulled her head to his chest. Adrian slowly raised her head and looked into his eyes.

"I cannot allow anyone to threaten your safety," she stated coldly. "Let them come to you, I will slaughter them at the gates," she added growling.

A slight smile crossed Christian's lips as he was pleased in her intentions. Though she was a force to be reckoned with, she was still a new Vampire. He felt if anyone would need protection, it would be her.

"I am joining you, William and Frederick this evening," she announced as she walked into the closet to retrieve her own clothing for the evening. "We have the upper hand, as they do not know I have returned," she added.

He knew she was right. He also knew any objection would prove to be futile. He proceeded to shower and dress for the meeting, and soon after they departed the suite arm-in-arm.

Chapter Twenty-Three

Halfway down the stairs they were met by the pups, who apparently had been misbehaving, as Sarah rushed behind them swinging a hand towel. Adrian stopped at the bottom of the stairs with the pups peeking at Sarah from behind her legs.

"What have they done?" she asked laughingly.

Sarah struggled to catch her breath and explained, "The pups have discovered the pantry," she smirked. "The galley is a complete disaster" she announced.

Christian and Adrian both fought the urge to laugh, as Sarah was quite flustered by the event. "I will keep watch over them for the remainder of the evening."

"I'm so sorry that they have caused such an uproar," Adrian apologized.

Sarah nodded and retreated to the kitchen.

Adrian and Christian turned and looked at the pups, "Bad children!" Adrian scolded as Christian laughed under his breath.

The moment of levity now behind them, they proceeded to Christian's study to meet with William and Frederick who were awaiting them. William lifted his head as they entered; surprised to see Adrian, they both stood to receive her.

"Good evening gentlemen," she responded as she motioned for them to return to their seats.

"What have we found?" Christian inquired, as he sat across the room from them, next to Adrian and the pups. Frederick squirmed in his seat as William began his report.

"We have received word Lucas called a meeting last night. It appears that over two dozen were present and expressed their desire to support him in his efforts. We are over fifty clans strong in supporters of our cause, Lord Christian," Frederick blurted.

"Battle ready if need be," William added.

Christian sighed heavily and fell back into the couch, "I had hoped it would not come to this; however, all evidence shows they are plotting that course."

"I say, let them come!" Adrian voiced. "We are the main ones who planned the defense of the Grenoble estate. I am confident we can do the same here!" she added.

"That is a certainty, with you at our defense Ms. Adrian," William said.

Adrian smiled at his comment before continuing, "We should call in the heads of security, brief them and begin fortifying the estate, as we did in Grenoble," she announced.

"Call a meeting for all new members and supporters of our cause," Christian chimed in. "I will meet with the security heads myself this evening.

"Frederick, deal with arming them.

"William, have all of our supporters meet here tomorrow evening for a briefing," he finished.

William and Frederick excused themselves, as they seemed eager to begin their tasks. Christian lifted the phone and called for the heads of Security to meet with him immediately. Everyone was now focused on their tasks.

Adrian remained on the couch with the pups and began to plot her lines of defense as well. Her deep thoughts were soon disturbed by the heads of Security as they entered the parlor.

"Good evening," they said in unison.

"I'm taking the dogs for a walk," she announced upon their entrance. She kissed Christian lightly on the cheek and summoned the pups to follow her, while they discussed security measures.

"Good evening Markus," she called as she exited the estate.

"Good evening Ms. Adrian. May I take you somewhere this evening?" he asked.

"Not at the moment, just walking the dogs," she smiled in return.

Adrian followed the pups to a large grove of oak trees and sat on the bench beneath them. The pups frolicked around her, excited to have her all to themselves. She became so engrossed in watching them play she had not noticed a car at the gate.

Sheba was the first to sense trouble; she sat erect with her ears pointed upward and began to growl in the direction of the car. Caesar soon followed suit. Adrian stood up from the bench as she began to feel a sense of dread washing over her. It was the same feeling she had when she saw the two men leaving the estate just the past evening.

Slowly, she moved behind one of the majestic tree trunks to observe them while remaining out of sight. The gate had now opened, and the long black car proceeded to the front entrance. Adrian began to focus on Christian to alert him of their presence. She watched as the same two men climbed from the back seat of the car. There was a brief flash as the second man rose. Adrian realized it was a sword that had caught the reflection of the full moon as he stood up.

Adrenaline now rushing through her body, she sped closer to the front entrance, still unnoticed by the two men. She watched as Christian exited the estate to meet them, her eyes fixed on the sword. She could see he had engaged the first of the two men in conversation, and knew that he was growing anxious with whatever was being said.

Their conversation was ended abruptly as Christian began shouting at them to leave. As he raised his hand and pointed toward the gate, the second man primed to swing the sword. Adrian sped up behind him and removed his head in one fatal swoop. His body fell to her feet as she stood hissing, still holding his head in her hand.

Adrian now turned to face his associate, her fangs bared and ready for his next move. He glared at her; furious with her actions, he bared his fangs back at her in rebuttal.

Adrian waited for him to pounce. Just as he lunged at her, Christian grabbed him from behind, twisted his neck and began to bleed him dry. Adrian rushed forward and held his arms down as she sank her fangs into him and fed as well. As the last of his blood was drained, Christian threw his limp corpse into the back of their car.

Adrian then threw the other body on top of his. Slowly she walked around the car, opened the door and looked in at the driver, who was horrified by her bloodstained face.

"Take them back to where they came from, and deliver this message: You have started a war that you will not win. Surrender now, or face certain death!" she said, as she slammed the car door.

The driver sped away and was out of sight within moments.

Frederick and William rushed to the front entrance, as they had heard the tires squeal. "What has happened?" William exclaimed, as his eyes scanned Christian and Adrian, both blood-soaked from their encounter.

"We are at war once more," Christian growled, as he held his arm out for Adrian to accompany him. "Markus, could you round up the pups for me?" Adrian called over her shoulder, as they entered the foyer.

"Yes, Miss," he replied, as he wandered off to retrieve them.

Christian paced the cold marble floors as he explained what had just happened. William and Frederick listened attentively as he spoke. There was now a thick silence in the room as they digested the situation. Frederick spoke first.

"We must begin to reinforce the estate immediately" he said. "I have contacted everyone as well about the meeting tomorrow night; all will be present" William added.

"There is much to do," Adrian added.

Markus walked into the parlor carrying the sword that had been intended to take Christian's head. She walked to Markus and took the sword from his hands. She began to slowly pace the room. Grasping its handle, soon she began to see where it had come from, as well as the men's intentions. Adrian spun around and looked into Christian's eyes.

"Lucas sent them," she scowled. "Had they been successful in their task, Lucas and his cohorts would be where we are standing now, as they were parked just outside of the gate," she added.

"Had I known this, I would have slaughtered them at that very moment," she growled. "I want to go after them," she demanded.

Christian walked over to her and placed his arms on her shoulders. "I understand; however, it is best to let them come to us for many reasons - most of all, politically," he finished.

Adrian attempted to calm herself, as she knew that his political position was important to him and at this point, extremely fragile.

She handed the sword to him and crossed the room to sit on the couch, where the pups had been waiting for her. Their noses twitched with curiosity; they began to climb upon her, licking at the blood that she still wore from earlier. Realizing how she must look, she excused herself in order clean up and change clothes.

Adrian grew angrier as she ascended the stairs. Again they had threatened her and Christian! They were the very root of the insurmountable pain that she and Christian had been subjected to. "I fought for them! I protected them! This will not happen again!" she vowed, as she held the door open for the pups to join her.

Adrian continued to pace the length of the room, she could sense that Lucas was still nearby; she could nearly smell him. She knew that he was reorganizing, preparing for a larger offensive. She became frenzied with rage.

Unable to fight the urge within her any longer, Adrian opened the window and jumped out onto the lawn. She sped across the grounds, over the fence, then down the rural winding highway as she tracked him. She had run several miles down the winding road before stopping suddenly.

Adrian looked to the sky as she filled her lungs with the cool night air. Her eyes sprung open; she had caught his scent, along with several others had accompanied him. "They are near" she whispered aloud.

She closed her eyes and began to rise from the ground, allowing the scent to draw her in their direction. Within moments, she found herself hovering over a small cottage that was tucked away far back into the thick woods. The cabin was alit and in front of it sat two limousines.

Adrian grinned. She could discern the scent of three Vampires and four sets of heartbeats. She looked down to see two guards walking from opposite sides of the cottage moving in her direction. "Two down," she smirked as she pounced down from her position.

Before her feet touched the ground, Adrian reached out and grabbed both men by the heads, smashing them into each other as she landed. Quickly, before their hearts stopped, she fed upon them, as she would need the strength for what would come next.

She discarded the bodies into the tree line and awaited her next opportunity, which nearly caught her off guard. The cabin door swung open to reveal another of the guards walking onto the front porch to light a cigarette.

Adrian rushed across the porch, swept him from his feet and snapped his neck, throwing him onto the other two bodies. As the body landed, she could hear chatter over his radio; she leaned over to retrieve it, and realized that she could hear the conversation inside of the cottage.

Just as she increased the volume, she heard Lucas growl, "They must both be destroyed! They are far too dangerous to exist amongst us!" he hissed. "Christian is intent on destroying the political process and Adrian is too young of a Vampire to possess the power that she has!" he seemed to become more agitated the longer that he spoke. "If we continue to allow them to run rampant they will ruin what we have fought for centuries to maintain," he demanded.

Adrian became furious and threw the radio into the woods. The rage within her boiled to a volatile point as she recalled the night that she, Naomi and Ruth had dragged Lucas and Christian from the caverns. He in such critical condition owed his existence to her many times over and now he stood just feet from her as he plotted her demise. Having heard more than enough of his ranting, Adrian clenched her fists and rushed into the cottage, blowing the door off of its hinges.

Immediately, she grabbed the last of the humans and snapped his neck, while her eyes were locked onto Lucas'. As she dropped his body to the floor, she slowly began to approach him. "How dare you plot against us, when not so long ago I saved your miserable lives, especially you!" she hissed.

The third of the Vampires, whom she did not know, began to lunge toward her. Adrian threw her hand up and slung him into the ceiling, willing him there while she continued to slowly approach Lucas. The Vampire struggled to loose himself from the unseen force, further infuriating her. She could feel a wave of adrenaline fueled by anger building within her. She focused herself and pushed her anger into the struggling Vampire; his skin began to melt from his bones.

Lucas, shocked by her display of power, was now backing away. Suddenly the third vampire walked slowly from the shadows of the hallway. Thomas moved slowly as he hoped to reason with her upon his approach. Lucas now stood frozen as Adrian redirected her gaze at him. "I loved you and you turned your back on me. You abandoned Christian in his time of need. What justification do you have for me to spare your life?" she growled.

Thomas began to speak, "Miss Adrian, if you would allow for me . . ." Adrian spun her head in his direction and flung him across the room before he could finish his opening line.

Lucas, seeing she was distracted, sprang at her, gashing her across her chest. His claws burned as they sliced through her. Momentarily distracted by her wounds, Thomas and Lucas began to close in on her. She watched from the corner of her eyes as she held her wound and doubled over. Just as they had gotten within her arm's reach, Adrian retaliated, spinning furiously and slicing both of their throats in one motion. Quickly, she pulled Lucas to her, and sank her fangs into his neck as he bled out. Thomas clutched at his throat in disbelief as he crawled towards her in a futile attempt to save Lucas.

Adrian dropped Lucas to the floor as the last of his blood drained from him, allowing him just enough time to witness Thomas' death before his life force would leave him. She sneered as his empty eyes gazed up at her then turned and lunged at Thomas, removing his head from his body in one clean blow. She looked about the cottage; seeing no movement, other than Thomas' twitching corpse, as a safety measure she decided to remove Lucas' head as well; they would make wonderful trophies for Christian, she thought, as she carried them out of the cottage. She threw the heads into the first car and drove back to the estate.

Markus was surprised to see Adrian climb from the car, as he had never seen her leave. William, Frederick and Christian were all arriving at the door; they had been notified by the gate guardsmen of a car as it had approached.

They stood defensively as she opened the door to get out. "What the hell are you doing?" Christian stammered as she stood, "My God, you're a mess! What happened," he asked.

Adrian walked around the car, still clutching at her wounds. "It's a long story, I have something for you," she smiled slyly. She opened the car door and retrieved the heads tossing them onto the ground at their feet.

William and Frederick gasped as Christian stood and stared blankly at them. Adrian leaned against the car to rest as she studied their expressions. The pups, now sensing her return, were leaning out of the window, barking down at her.

Christian looked up at the open window and back to Adrian; just then, he realized that she had been wounded. Panicking, he swept her up and into the parlor. "How bad is it?" he asked, as he sat down with her in his lap.

"Not very, it just burns a bit," she answered. Christian lifted her blouse to inspect the injury, then opened his wrist to drip his blood onto her wound and speed her healing. He leaned and kissed her softly on her cheek just as William and Frederick entered the room.

"How is she?" Frederick asked.

"I'm fine," she said as they approached her. The room became quiet momentarily, while their shock at her actions sank in.

"Adrian, I know you are exhausted but you must tell me what happened," Christian coaxed. Just as the words had left his mouth, Sarah rushed into the room.

"Markus told me Miss Adrian has been wounded!" she panted.

"I'm fine, Sarah, nothing a glass of wine won't fix," she chuckled.

"Right away," Sarah responded, as she hustled from the room.

Adrian propped herself upon the couch and began to explain in detail what had happened since she left them earlier. There had been a deep sense of dread and concern in the room, until she told them of her overhearing Lucas and Thomas plotting to kill her and Christian. With all of the events of the evening relayed, there was now an eerie but lighthearted feel in the room.

Sarah had returned with her glass of wine, while Christian poured drinks for everyone else. Adrian sipped at her wine and then examined her wounds to see that she was completely healed.

"Shall I help you clean up, Ms. Adrian?" Sarah asked.

"No, thank you Sarah," she responded realizing that she must be a sight. Sarah stood wringing her hands, as she could not stand to see her mistress covered in filth. Adrian giggled at her.

"Christian will help me to the suite in a moment," she added in order to ease Sarah's mind. "Yes, Miss," Sarah nodded as she left the room.

Adrian took another sip of her wine and asked Christian to escort her upstairs. Christian, obliging, excused them for the remainder of the evening so that they could focus on the task of preparing for another possible attack. He lifted her from the couch and carried her up the stairs and to the suite, putting her down in the chair near the tub.

"You are a sight!" he laughed. Adrian stood and approached the mirror. She was horrified at the creature stared back at her. Every inch of her was coated in now-hardened blood and body tissue; her pale blue eyes stared back at her from behind the gory mask she wore.

"Oh my God," she whispered, as she continued to stare in horror.

Christian, sensing that she was becoming upset, decided to distract her, "Here, let me help you," he said as he approached her and began to remove her filthy clothes.

Adrian fought to control her rogue emotions. Exhaustion combined with death and deception had rendered her into an agitated state. Christian, sensing the ongoing battle within her offered his arm to her and ushered her to the shower. He removed his clothes and joined her in order to help her clean herself. She stood submissively as he gently washed her; she stared at the drain as the blood streaming from her body turned the water into a thick dark crimson sludge that swirled its' way down the drain beneath her. It seemed that the water would never run clear again.

Eventually, Christian turned off the shower, wrapped her in a towel and carried her to the bed, where the pups lay anxiously waiting for her. "I love you" Christian said, as he stood back to admire his work.

"I know" she replied, as he turned to retrieve a towel for himself. "Great ass!" Adrian called after him as he walked away. She could see him grinning as he passed in front of the vanity mirror.

Christian returned wrapped in a towel and sat on the bed beside her. "What kind of retribution will this bring upon us?" Adrian asked.

Christian sighed and sat beside her on the bed. "Who knows?" he shrugged. "It may have stopped this impending war, or it may bring one that was coming anyway," he finished.

"I assume this will definitely expose our enemies," Adrian added. She sat up in the bed and straddled him from behind, placed her chin upon his shoulder, and held him. "I could not let them threaten us again," she whispered into his ear.

Christian wrapped his arms around hers. "I could not agree more," he said, as he turned to face her.

He placed a passionate kiss upon her lips and stroked her naked thigh. Adrian melted at his touch. The inner battle that she was hosting seemed to come to a halt, surrendering to her overwhelming emotions for Christian. She slid around to face him, now straddling his lap as she returned his passionate kiss with one of her own.

Slowly, she slid from his lap until she was on her knees in front of him. She removed his towel to expose his already-throbbing cock. She gently slid it into her mouth and sucked at him as she stroked him with her lips. She had forgotten how much pleasure she found in making love to him. Within moments, Christian pulled her back up into his lap and inserted himself into her. He stood with her in his arms as she wrapped her legs around him.

Christian walked across the room and braced her back against the wall as he slowly plunged himself into her. Adrian spread her legs wide as she balanced her weight on his broad shoulders; within moments, she was in full orgasm. Christian wedged himself firmly into her as he pulled her hips down tightly upon him. Adrian sank her nails into his back as she called out for him; as her climax began to decline, Christian carried them back to the bed and began to slowly make love to her.

Within moments she was at climax once more. She wrapped her arms around his back and pulled him further into her, prompting him into orgasm as well. Adrian rocked her hips frantically to lengthen his ecstasy, as he clutched at her ass and exploded into her. Moments later they collapsed in exhaustion, sated from their lovemaking.

They slept peacefully throughout the day.

Chapter Twenty-Four

Adrian woke just before sunset to find Christian was not in bed beside her. She assumed he was downstairs meeting with William and Frederick about security issues, and decided to take a long hot bath before joining them.

As she submerged herself into the steaming water, she began to reflect upon her actions the previous night. "A year ago, I could have killed someone to save myself or someone I love. Last night, I took eight lives out of anger" she thought to herself. She worried she might not be able to hold onto her humanity much longer. She wondered if the guards that she had killed had families of their own; had she taken a father or a husband from someone?

Her mortal thoughts were in direct conflict with her Vampire instincts; her mind was a blur. What was she becoming? Was there any way to balance compassion with the fierce creature that lurked within her?

Christian was compassionate towards her when she was human, but he had also told her the story of his vengeance for Cassandra, proving that he was also a fierce Vampire. She decided to give up on her thoughts and get dressed to go downstairs and meet up with Christian.

She stood from the tub to dress for the evening. Now ready to join Christian, she headed to the door. She found it odd that the shutter was still in place. She flipped the switch to raise the steel shutter, nothing happened. She flipped it once more; still the shutter remained closed tight. "What the fuck?" she mumbled as she continued to flip the switch.

"Fine," she sighed, as she walked to the window. "I'll go the long way," she thought, as she flipped the lever for the shutter over the window to be released. Once again, nothing happened; the shutter remained sealed tight.

Adrian walked to the phone to call downstairs. She lifted the handset to her ear to find that the line was dead.

Adrian was becoming anxious and called out for Christian. She could not feel him around her. As a matter of fact, she could not sense him at all. "What the hell is going on?" she asked aloud.

She rushed across the room and dug her cell phone from her purse. She dialed Christian first. No answer. Then Markus - no answer. Lastly she dialed the estate phone number. Once again, there was no answer.

"What the fuck?" she yelled. Adrian was now becoming panicked. "Christian, where are you?" she called out to him.

She began to look around the room for something to try to pry the shutters loose, to no avail. She studied the wall around the door and decided to try and claw her way through it. She began digging through the sheetrock and wall coverings, only to find a solid stone wall behind them. Surely the exterior walls would be the same, she thought, as she looked to the floor.

She dropped to her knees and began clawing her way through the floor. As she removed the first few pieces of wood, she heard the shutter begin to raise on the door. She had made enough noise to let someone know she was locked in, or so she thought.

Adrian stood as she waited to thank whoever had come to her rescue. The shutter barely opened before four guards pounced onto her, covering her with a silver mesh net; she had been caught off guard.

Her skin burned and smoked; the pain was unbearable. She screamed out for Christian, to no avail. She fought viciously to free herself from the net. As she struggled, her flesh was being ripped from her body everywhere that the silver touched her. She was rapidly beginning to weaken.

William and Frederick both now entered the room. Frederick knelt down beside her. "Not so fierce now, are we?" he smirked. "We just can't go around killing other elders, Miss Adrian," William now mocked at her.

She was in so much pain from the silver that it was all she could do to comprehend what they were saying to her.

"Where is Christian?" she hissed at them.

"Don't worry about Christian, he's in safekeeping," Frederick smirked. "Lock her down!" he ordered as he walked from the room.

The guards then lifted her to her feet and carried her down the stairs into the basement level of the estate. She had never experienced such agony.

They dragged her to a small dank cell comprised of concrete with a barred door made of pure silver. The guards slung her free of the net and into the cell. She went crashing into the opposite wall and slid to the floor. She curled herself into a fetal position, shivering with pain as her skin smoldered.

Moments later Frederick and William arrived in front of the cell, "Why are you doing this?" she moaned, as they sneered down at her.

"We believe in preserving the Vampire nation as it always has been," William answered as he spat upon the floor at her feet. "You are an abomination, a new Vampire with the blood of elders pulsing through your veins. He created you and began the ruination of the Parliament. For this he will be punished, and you will be dealt with as well," he grinned.

Adrian could feel anger building within her, but was physically too weak to direct it towards them.

"Fuck you both," she said as she turned her head to face the cold damp wall.

Frederick and William laughed as they left her trembling in her prison cell. She sat quietly and listened until she couldn't hear their footsteps any longer.

Adrian began to inspect her wounds as she attempted to focus on Christian. She could feel him now, and sensed that he was very weak. "Where are you?" she called out to him.

She could hear him faintly answer her, "I don't know, it's dark here and I am confined."

"I'm locked in a cell beneath the estate," she said; there came no reply. Adrian began to worry over his condition and searched the cell to look for any weak areas in the wall or door to escape from. Having examined the interior thoroughly, she came to the conclusion the best opportunity she would have is to focus on the lock of her cell door.

Adrian feebly rose to her knees and cleared her mind of all the pain and turmoil that was within her. She opened her eyes and began to concentrate on the lock. The longer she stared into it, the more drained she became. Adrian began to lose her patience and in a fit of rage she swung her arms out towards the door and fell back to the floor. The door flew from its hinges and landed across the corridor from her cell.

Fearing that the crash would bring guards to investigate, she pooled her remaining strength and moved swiftly through the corridors until she found her way to the hangar.

Quietly, she moved to the front of the hangar, knowing that there would be security stationed out front and she would need to feed in order to heal and build her strength. Adrian stood behind the door and opened it slightly, waiting for someone to investigate.

Almost immediately, a guard approached and stepped inside. Just as he reached for his radio to relay his position, she slammed the door behind him and tackled him, removing his weapon from his grasp.

Adrian struggled to restrain him as she sank her fangs into his neck. She drained him completely and hid the limp body in a small storage room just left of the doorway.

"Where are you, Christian?" she called out as she watched her wounds begin to close. No answer came.

She continued to call out to him as she stepped behind the door to attempt her ploy once more. She opened the door and heard two guards approaching. As they entered the hangar, she pounced, tackling both of them to the floor, snapping one's spine immediately as she turned to drain the other. She dragged the two bodies into the same storage closet as the first and forced the door closed.

"Christian, where are you?" she called out again. She could not feel his presence anywhere and worried if he was still alive.

Adrian felt completely restored and now was angry. With vengeance pulsing through her veins, she left the hangar and made her way back to the estate. Several guards were encountered along the way; Adrian fed well on them.

She ran to the west wall of the estate and held her palm to the stone wall, searching for any indication that Christian was inside. Her anger was now maddening, compounded by the lack of response from Christian. She was now determined to search the estate for him.

The shutters were all sealed tightly. There was no way for her to reenter the estate without alerting William and Frederick of her presence. Adrian looked up at the roof; sure to be guarded, it still seemed to be her best option. Stealthily, she climbed the west wall just as two guards patrolled below her.

Now at the roof line, she slowly peered over the wall, noting one man on the far corner and two at the stair entrance. Adrian scaled around the roof line until she was directly under the guard at the corner. She sprang from the wall and pulled him down by his neck.

The man struggled as he hung from her grip, unable to fill his lungs with enough air to scream. She clung to him until his body ceased to twitch then dropped him into the shrubbery down below. She scanned the grounds behind her. Satisfied she had not been spotted, she sprang from the wall once more, tackling the two remaining guards at the entrance. She twisted their heads until their necks snapped then dropped them over the wall to join their friend.

Adrian took a deep breath as she approached the door, not knowing what she would face once she walked through it. Slowly, she pushed the door open, to find the hallway abandoned. Relieved, she quietly moved down the hallway towards the main stairs. She listened attentively for any movement on the lower level, where she knew that all hell would certainly be unleashed.

Adrian peered around the wall to the lower level, which was eerily silent. With no one in sight, she sped down the stairs then ducked behind the foyer wall. She could hear voices in the distance; they seemed to be originating from behind the chamber doors. She was perplexed by the absence of activity on the main level.

Was this a trap or was it a blatant display of their arrogance? Adrian closed her eyes and attempted to contact Christian once more. Though she got no response from him, she was able to sense that he was near. She grew frantic, as she could only imagine what they may have done to him.

She began to make her way down the hallway and stopped just before the chamber doors, confirming that the voices were coming from inside. Adrian remembered the sword

CHAPTER TWENTY-FOUR PAGE 188

from the previous evening and sped into the parlor adjacent to her in hopes that it was still there.

She glanced around the room and was pleased to find the sword lying across the desk where Christian had placed it previously. Adrian gripped the handle tightly and turned to make her entrance.

Now back in front of the immense wooden doors of the chambers, she pushed lightly on them to see if they had been barred from inside. The door moved slightly at her touch.

She backed away and then charged through the doors with the sword drawn in front of her. Suddenly she slid to a stop. There before her hung Christian, clad in silver chains, with a dagger in his chest. Adrian fell to her knees at the sight. She wailed as his body gently swung back and forth, the last of his blood dripping slowly to the floor beneath him.

She was so grief-stricken that she had not noticed the bodies of his guards that lined the floors nor William and Frederick, who were seated across the room from her.

Frederick was the first to speak, "Are you enjoying this as thoroughly as I?" he said to William smugly, as he shifted in his seat. William uncrossed his legs, grinning wildly as he gloated, "This is a moment that I shall cherish for eternity," he responded as he stood.

William walked smugly towards Adrian, who was struggling to get to her feet. He stopped before he reached her and looked up at Christian's remains, "Sad," he sighed, as he pushed against Christian's legs, causing him to swing violently.

Suddenly, both he and Frederick appeared in front of her. Dazed from the grief welling inside of her, she was unprepared for their attack. They lunged at her simultaneously, tackling her to the floor. She struggled beneath them as they clawed at her and sank their fangs into her flesh. Adrian fought to keep them from pinning her arms. William, becoming irritated with her, rose up and struck her in the face, slicing her open with his blow.

Frederick was now restraining her legs as he bit into her right thigh. She howled in pain as he tore at her with his fangs.

William wrapped his hands around her neck and squeezed with all of his might. His lips curled as he leered down into her face, "Tonight you die whore," he growled, as he wrenched on her neck. Adrian gazed up as Christian's mangled body swung over her.

Through the chaos there was silence and she heard his voice, "Adrian, concentrate. You must not suffer my fate. You are stronger than they are."

The silence had given way to chaos once more; she clenched her fists and turned her pain into rage. She broke her arms free from William's grasp and pulled his face down to her. She dug her fangs into his cheek, ripping his flesh from his face as she kicked Frederick from her legs.

Rage fueled her to stand, grasping William by the throat, she drew him face-to-face with her. She glared into his eyes and released her pain into him. William began to writhe in agony as the shock on his face shifted into terror. He began to twitch as she tightened her grip on his throat.

Frederick, now back on his feet, lunged towards her.

Adrian lifted her free hand, directing her anger upon him, flung him across the room once more.

Now returning her attention to William, she rammed her hand into his chest, pulling his heart out as she retracted. William fell to the ground as Adrian turned to face Frederick, who was once again struggling to stand.

Adrian dropped William's now shriveled heart onto the floor before her and began to approach Frederick. He, now regaining his foothold, stood to defend himself.

Adrian was maddened with rage. She held her hand out before him and focused her energy into him.

"No," he begged, as he sank back to his knees.

Adrian continued to leer at him. His begging only infuriated her further. Frederick was now bleeding from all orifices. She continued to force her will onto him as the last of his blood spilled onto the floor about him.

The chamber grew silent once more, with the exception of the groaning chain that Christian's remains swung from. Adrian hesitated before she turned to face the gruesome display. Her eyes pointed to the floor, she turned towards him, rose to the rafters and released him. His body fell to the floor below. Adrian, now beside him placed her hands on what was once his beautiful face; his burned skin crumbled away at her touch.

Her heart felt as though it would explode within her as she rested her head upon his still smoldering chest. She sobbed with all that remained within her. Her release of emotions had a strange effect upon her; instead of being weakened, she could feel the energies within her surging.

Adrian raised her head from Christian and screamed with all of her might. The crystal chandeliers above her began to shatter, as did all the glass fixtures throughout the estate. Her howling droned on through the marble halls of the estate; she could hear crashing all about her.

Adrian's screams had silenced now as she looked down at Christian's remains. She gathered her strength and lifted his fragile corpse from the floor and began to carry him from the chambers.

As she willed the doors open before her, the remaining staff began to gather into the hallway. She looked up to see Markus, who immediately began to weep at the loss of his master. Several of his loyal staff rushed to assist her with carrying his body; she hissed at them as a warning not to interfere.

Adrian trudged to the front entrance as the staff filed in line behind her. Markus flipped the switch to raise the shutters as she approached. The sky told of a coming sunrise as the doors opened with a thud. She winced as she stepped out of the grand entrance and onto the bloodied dew-soaked front lawn, the remaining staff in tow.

After a few steps she realized that there were still guards present. She stopped in her tracks preparing to defend herself. The guards saw that she was carrying Christian's remains. Knowing that the battle was over, they shouldered their weapons and began to leave the grounds. Adrian nodded as she continued to the centuries-old cemetery just beyond the estate grounds.

There, in the center of the modest burial grounds, amongst the dated headstones, stood a large marble mausoleum. Adrian stopped at the wrought iron fence that embraced the cold white crypt. Markus scurried to the gate to open it for her. He bowed his head as she approached the large stone slab that blocked the doorway.

Adrian focused on the barricade. Her body trembled as the large stone moved to grant her access. She began to move forward once more, then stopped as she neared Markus.

Still facing the now-beckoning opening of the tomb, she spoke. "I trust you will take care of Christian's estate in my absence" she said numbly.

Markus wore a baffled expression upon his face, but agreed. "Of course, Miss Adrian" he affirmed, as he sniffed away his tears while nodding.

Adrian, still facing forward, returned his nod then walked into the mausoleum.

The remnants of his loyal staff stood watching on as their hearts filled with grief. Adrian turned as she crossed the entrance and looked out into their mourning faces.

"At last we will know peace," she said as she disappeared into the darkness.

The weary staff, confused by her statement, continued to peer into the crypt. Moments later the massive stone slid back in place, sealing the tomb from inside for eternity.

About the Author

A true "Southern Belle" was born in Jefferson Parish and now resides in Southeast Louisiana. Having enlisted in the United States Military upon graduation, Lyn chose to apply her newly earned discipline and management skills towards a career.

From the early 1980's, until present, Lyn developed an extensive background in upper level management ranging from night clubs to the largest real estate brokerage in Southeastern Louisiana, while also holding the Chairperson's position at the Regional Real Estate Board.

As a multi-faceted individual, Lyn finds time to dabble in many areas of art. Painting, stone masonry and writing are all favorite past-times as well as a deep love of all things associated with local folklore and legend.

Always having had a deep interest in the paranormal, writing a novel was a future plan.

In 2011, Lyn penned, "To Be His Soulmate" and self-published prior to approaching her publisher, dpInk: Donnalnk Publications, L.L.C. formerly the Book Nook / Donnalnk Publications (a sole proprietorship). *To Be His Soulmate* was re-editioned and re-released. It was followed by Volume II, *Adrian's Fury*, which you have just read.

Volume III, *Adrian's Legacy* follows *Adrian's Fury* fall of 2014 prior to the holiday season. *Adrian's Legacy* completes *The Adrian Trilogy* series.

In 2015, a new title, *Short and Gory* is being released at the onset of summertime!

Visit the Author

Publisher

DonnaInk Publications, L.L.C: http://www.donnaink.com

Social Media

Facebook: https://www.facebook.com/AuthorLynGibson

Twitter: @AuthorLynGibson

WordPress Blog: http://authorlyngibson.wordpress.com

Website

http://www.authorlyngibson.com

Mailing List and Merchandise

In order to become aware of discounts, events, interviews, signings and promotion campaign activities remit an email to: theadriantrilogy@donnaink.com and put "Mailing List" in the subject line. Some of Ms. Gibson's publisher sponsored merchandise includes:

dpInk

Donnalnk Publications, L.L.C.
www.donnaink.org

Publisher
www.donnaink.com

For bulk orders, special orders, etc.

Special Markets Division
dpInk: Donnalnk Publications, L.L.C.
129 Daisy Hill Road
Carthage, North Carolina 28327
Email: special_markets@donnaink.com

For Promotions:
Promotions Division
dpInk: Donnalnk Publications, L.L.C.
129 Daisy Hill Road
Carthage, North Carolina 28327
Email: promotions@donnaink.com

ZENCON ART OF
ZEN CONSULTANCY
PR & Marketing

www.ingramcontent.com/pod-product-compliance
Lightning Source LLC
Chambersburg PA
CBHW060540210326
41519CB00014B/3293